A Woman's Journey through Luke

12 Lessons on The Savior
Exclusively for Women

Dee Brestin

Chariot Victor Publishing
A Division of Cook Communications

Titles by Dee Brestin

From Chariot Victor
The Friendships of Women
The Friendships of Women Workbook
We Are Sisters
The Joy of Hospitality
The Joy of Women's Friendships
The Joy of Eating Right
A Woman of Joy
A Woman of Value
A Woman of Insight
A Woman's Journey through Luke
A Woman's Journey through Ruth
A Woman's Journey through Esther

Fisherman Bible Study Guides
(Harold Shaw Publishers)
Proverbs and Parables
Ecclesiastes
Examining the Claims of Christ (John 1–5)
1, 2 Peter and Jude
How Should a Christian Live? (1, 2, 3 John)
Higher Ground
Building Your House on the Lord
Friendship

From Moody Press
Believer's Lifesystem—Women's Edition Bible Study

Chariot Victor Publishing
A division of Cook Communications, Colorado Springs, Colorado 80918
Cook Communications, Paris, Ontario
Kingsway Communications, Eastbourne, England

Editor: Barbara Williams
Design: Bill Gray
Cover Photo: Kevin Buckley

Luke describes more incidents involving women
than any other Gospel writer.
Here, Luke writes: "They laughed at Him,
knowing that she was dead.
But He took her by the hand and said,
"My child, get up!" (Luke 8:53-54)

Contents

How I Thank God For:

Dr. Darrell L. Bock of Dallas Seminary
Whose award-winning commentaries on Luke are the best I have ever used and have profoundly impacted this guide.

Whose support and counsel in reading and commenting upon this manuscript has been of inestimable value to me and to the women doing this study.

The Team at Chariot Victor in Colorado Springs
Who are showing unusual faith by setting the price of this guide low so that it could be available to more women. How we need publishers like you!

Particularly Greg Clouse (for his discernment and efficacy) and Barb Williams (for her eye for detail).

My Team at Home in Nebraska
Particularly Gay Tillotson for dozens of vital tasks done well and enthusiastically.

The reflective and diligent women in my Sonrise Bible Study for testing this study and then vulnerably allowing me to read their answers.

My Precious Family

Introduction

Vickie Kraft, a pioneer in women's ministries, discovered that her male students at Dallas Seminary frequently illustrated their sermons with anecdotes about cars, sports, or the military. She exhorted them to become more sensitive to women. For while it *is* true that men and women have much in common, there are also some key differences, for God made us male and female. Elisabeth Elliot says, "The soul of a woman is feminine." We are not less valuable than men, as Jesus makes abundantly clear (particularly in Luke!) by the way He treated us, but we are different. And both men and women are discovering the value of studying at times exclusively with their own gender.

Luke is *particularly* empathetic to women. In Luke alone we read the details of the actual birth of Christ. As his Gospel continues, there are many incidents *unique* to Luke which are of great interest to women, such as the story of Mary and Martha. Why? Luke tells us he received his historical account from eyewitnesses. Who were those eyewitnesses? The apostles—definitely. But historians consider the possibility that Luke received much of his information from Mary, the mother of Jesus, and from the devout company of women who traveled with the Twelve and helped to support them out of their means (Luke 8:1-3). Why do I, as a woman, identify with so many passages in Luke? Perhaps it is because women may have been a primary source. Perhaps it is because Luke shows so clearly how Jesus valued women, reached out to women, used women for vital messages, and understood women's deepest longings.

We will also be approaching this book differently than men might. Men often feel a successful journey means covering a lot of territory rapidly, getting an overview and skipping the details! I remember a whirlwind trip I took with my dear dad through England, Scotland, and Wales. The week is a blur in my memory except for one day when I persuaded Dad to slow down and spend the *whole* day exploring Oxford and the places significant to C.S. Lewis. We walked along the hill Lewis was on when he was converted, we sat in halls in which he taught, we lunched in a pub in which he debated theology, and we closed our day by standing at the headstone where his body was buried. That day is a golden memory, worth the price of the whole trip, and because of it, both C.S. Lewis and my dad are even more precious to me than before!

I don't want Luke's Gospel (or the women in your small group!) to be a blur in your memory. Though you will certainly have the opportunity through the Extra

Credit readings to drive through all of Luke, it is not required. It is required to stop, get out of the car (for we will stay several weeks at each of our four oasis stops), and ask God each day: "Father, please help me to see what You have for me today!"

Special Instructions for Preparation and Discussion

Once, while being interviewed, the Omaha radio announcer tried to provoke me by saying: "I doubt very much that any serious growth occurs in women's Bible studies—they are simply glorified kaffeeklatsches!" I was able to share with him (most graciously, of course) that, in my present study, the women had memorized John 15, had done their homework, and were sharing vulnerably, as many men are hesitant to do, from their hearts. Any gender can turn a study into a kaffeeklatsch, but there are certain standards you can set right now to prevent that:

1.   Do your homework! Each day, same time, same place, for a minimum of thirty minutes. Each day, ask God to speak to you through His Word. If you don't have a hymnal, buy one! Every home needs a Bible and a hymnal!
Certain hymns for your quiet times will be suggested.

2.   In the discussion, be sensitive to the Spirit. The naturally talkative need to exercise control and the shy need to exercise courage and speak up.

3.   Stay on target in the discussions. These lessons can be discussed in ninety minutes. If you don't have that much time, you have two options:

    A. Divide the lessons. Do three days a week for twenty-four weeks. Do that week's prayer exercise both weeks.

    B. Do the whole lesson but discuss half the questions.

4.   Follow the instructions for group prayer at the close of each lesson. Keep confidences in the group. There is power when we pray together.

May you rejoice, as Mary did, in the realization that God is mindful of you (Luke 1:46-48).

THE SAVIOR'S BIRTH

So they hurried off and found Mary
and Joseph, and the baby, who was
lying in the manger.
—Luke 2:16

The Savior's Birth
(Luke 1–2)

The church of my childhood was not Bible-centered, though exceptions were made at Christmas and Easter. At Christmas, we always read the second chapter of Luke and sang carols based on this hauntingly beautiful passage. (Luke alone tells the intimate details of the birth.) Therefore, when I was confronted with the claims of Christ as a young wife and mother, I had to decide whether Jesus was a fairy tale or God incarnate. I prayed and cried out to God to show me the truth. The images which kept flooding my mind and which caused me to pursue the truth were the majestic scenes from the birth: the glory of the Lord shining around the terrified shepherds; the announcement of the sign: a baby wrapped in swaddling clothes and lying in a manger; and the angelic message: "Do not be afraid. I bring you good news of great joy! Today in the town of David a Savior has been born to you; He is Christ the Lord."

Since Luke's birth account was pivotal in bringing me to Christ, it is dear to me. But the longer I looked at this tapestry, the more I saw that touched me as a woman. The story begins tenderly with the births of two babies. First, John the Baptist. Then, the Christ Child. And, woven into this tapestry is also the account of the God-ordained friendship of their two mothers. Come with me to spend a few weeks at the oasis of "The Savior's Birth."

First Stop!
Blameless and Barren

*W*ho of us does not long for special friends to love and to be loved by? God knows our longings as women—for He is the One who created us to be the relational sex! He also brings friends across our path who can particularly minister to our unique needs and to whom we can minister. But we need to be alert, as Elizabeth was to Mary, and as Mary was to Elizabeth.

I would encourage you to be alert to the women in this small group—for God may have placed someone here especially with you in mind. Ask God to give you discernment. Author and speaker Win Couchman says: "Sometimes when I first meet an interesting woman I have a lust to acquire her as a friend—like a possession. But if I pray—God may completely change my attitude, and my motive becomes purer, or, I find myself drawn to a different woman!" So pray. Plead for discernment! God knows your needs better than you do.

In addition, notice that God is more likely to anoint those whose hearts are blameless toward Him and who are stepping out in faith. See how this is true in Elizabeth's life.

Prepare Your Heart to Hear
Before each of the following six devotional times, quiet your heart and ask God to speak to you personally from His Word.

Memory Work
In this birth oasis you will memorize Luke 1:46-50. This week begin with verses 46 and 47:

And Mary said: "My soul praises the Lord and my spirit rejoices in God my Savior."

Warm-Up

Share your name and why you came to this group. Was Jesus a part of your childhood Advents or Christmases? If so, what memory stands out?

Day 1: Overview

1. Read all of the introductory notes. Comment on what stood out to you from:
    A. The Introduction (p. 7)

    B. The special Instructions for Preparation and Discussion (p. 8)

    C. The Introduction for THE FIRST OASIS: THE SAVIOR'S BIRTH (p. 10)

    D. The Introduction for THE FIRST STOP! BLAMELESS AND BARREN (p. 11)

Read Luke 1.

As you read, see if you can think of someone you know who reminds you of each: Zechariah, Elizabeth, and Mary.

Spend five minutes on the memory passage.
Often doing a word at a time will help to cement it in your mind:
> Luke
> Luke 1
> Luke 1:46-50
> Luke 1:46-50 And
> Luke 1:46-50 And Mary . . .
> etc.

Day 2: Introducing Elizabeth, Blameless in God's Sight

Author Susan Hunt uses the words "spiritual mothering" instead of "mentoring." We are to nurture the younger women in our lives (Titus 2:3-5). We don't need to be as old as Elizabeth for all of us are older than someone. God longs to love and teach the younger women in our lives through us, but before He can do that, we need to be in an intimate relationship with Him.

2.   What evidences in Luke 1 do you find that imply Elizabeth knew and trusted God? Write down the verse and why you believe it shows an intimacy with God.

Elizabeth was blameless in God's sight. This does not mean that she was perfect but, as *The Message* paraphrases it, that she "enjoyed a clear conscience before God." This begins by coming to God in salvation, by putting our trust in the payment that God provided through Jesus on the cross. Isaiah 1:18 gives us the following word picture of what happens to a person in God's sight when he puts his trust in Christ:

> Though your sins are like scarlet,
> they shall be as white as snow.

3.   What do you learn about living a holy and "blameless" life from the following passages?

A. 1 John 1:7-9

B. Philippians 2:14-16

C. 1 Thessalonians 5:23

Day 3: Barren, but Trusting

My husband and I have not struggled with infertility, but our son John and daughter-in-law Julie struggled with bringing a baby to term. I never knew how much it hurt until it happened to us. One of the things I feared was that John and Julie would stop trusting God. They were trying to live wholeheartedly for Him—so why was this happening?

One day John said to me: "Mom, if God never gives us a baby, we will trust Him."

"Why?"

"Because He died for us."

How we need to remember this truth in dark times. Elizabeth probably came to the point in her life when she assumed she would never be a mother.

Was it because of sin in her life?

Was it because God did not love her?

Was it because God was not able to give her children?

No! No! No! Elizabeth was blameless and barren because God had a plan she could not see.

Like John and Julie, Elizabeth looked at the character of God and chose to trust Him in the dark.

Personal Reflection Only

As you are still before the Lord, is there anything that needs to go in order for you to enjoy a clear conscience before Him?

4.   In Luke 1, what two words beginning with "b" are used to describe Elizabeth? What does the juxtaposition of these two words teach you?

5.   Have you ever been or are you being denied a deep desire of your heart? Have you faced times when God did not make sense? What were your feelings?

What can you learn from saints of the past, like Job, Elizabeth, and others who trusted God in the dark?

6.   What do the following verses tell you about the character of God which could help you when He is not making sense?
    Λ. 1 Peter 5:7

    B. Ecclesiastes 3:11

Review your memory passage.

Horatio Spafford wrote the words to "It Is Well with My Soul" after surveying the place in the ocean where his four daughters drowned. Sing this hymn from your hymnal in your private devotional time.

Day 4: A Godly Wife

Some couples are in a negative cycle. One criticizes, the other responds in kind, and round it goes! Hearts harden in this kind of marriage. When Zechariah doubted God, we see no evidence of disrespect on Elizabeth's part. She seems to overlook his weakness in love. She believes in him and supports him.

Read Luke 1:6-25 again.

7.   What strengths and weaknesses do you see in Elizabeth's husband, Zechariah?

8.   How did God discipline Zechariah for the doubting words he spoke to Gabriel? What thoughts and feelings do you think Zechariah had as he was deaf and dumb for the following nine months?

Read Luke 1:57-80.

9.   Find clues in Luke 1:57-80 for:
     A. Elizabeth and Zechariah's positive relationship

B. Zechariah's teachable heart

10. What can a woman do to draw her husband closer to God? What mistakes do wives make which harden their husbands' hearts?

11. If you are married, what are some of the strengths you see in your husband? What godly characteristics? List them—and tell him about them today!

What are some ways you could help a close married friend to think well of her husband?

Read Matthew 1:18-25.

12. How did Joseph react similarly to Zechariah?

How did God help Joseph to believe?

13. Imagine that Mary confided in Elizabeth that Joseph was having trouble believing God. What reassuring words, based on her experience and faith, might Elizabeth have given to Mary?

Day 5: Filled with the Holy Spirit

Every day of my life I long for the power of the Holy Spirit: to hear from God in my quiet time; to respond to my loved ones as God would have me respond; to overcome sin; and to experience His power and wisdom in my ministries as a writer and speaker.

14. In the following cases which Luke reports, various things happened to believers who were filled with the Holy Spirit. What were they?
    A. Luke 1:41-45

    B. Luke 1:67

    C. Acts 2:4

    D. Acts 4:8-10

    E. Acts 4:31

    F. Acts 9:17

G. Acts 13:9-12

H. Acts 13:52

15. Believers receive the Holy Spirit when they put their trust in Christ (John 3:5; Romans 8:9), but believers continue to receive empowerment from Him by keeping a clear conscience (sin quenches the Spirit) and by stepping out in faith. How do you see these two aspects in the lives of Elizabeth and Zechariah?

Personal Action Assignment

Today, follow the example of Elizabeth. Keep a clear conscience by responding quickly to the Holy Spirit. Leave your journal open and record times you respond. For example:

> 7 A.M. Good quiet time—please, God, help me remember my "Walking in Faith Day"
> 10:30 A.M. Obeyed His prompting to write and encourage Aunt Helen
> 2:30 P.M. Turned difficult unanswered prayer over to God—I will trust Him as Elizabeth did in the dark
> 4 P.M. Yelled at Timmy for spilling milk. Asked forgiveness for my harshness from God and Timmy
> 7 P.M. Obeyed His prompting to read instead of watching television. Great day! Thank You, Lord

Meditate on Luke 1:39-45. (Read this aloud in the group.)

16. Describe what happened to Elizabeth.

17. Elizabeth could have been jealous of Mary who was carrying a baby of much greater importance than her own. Find evidence that Elizabeth was not jealous.

Why, in your opinion, wasn't Elizabeth jealous?

18. Elizabeth's humility, her desire to elevate Jesus, can be seen in Elizabeth's son as well. Give evidence for that based on Luke 3:15-17.

What evidence can others see in your life for your desire to elevate Jesus?

Review your memory verse.

Day 6: God Cared for Elizabeth

Jesus promises that if we put Him first, He will meet our needs (Luke 12:31). Elizabeth's five-month seclusion probably had a spiritual motive, as evidenced by Luke 1:25. Her first response was to seek God, rather than run to her friends.

In the first fifteen years of our marriage, my husband and I moved eight times. Each time we moved to a new city I asked God to give me a woman soul mate *right away*. He never did it *right away*. He knows my tendency as a woman to depend on people instead of Him! Instead, He always made me wait. When He saw that I was abiding in Him and, secondly, honoring my husband, then He would trust me with a woman soul mate.

19. Are you putting God first in your life? Are you seeking Him as Elizabeth did? Does your quiet time come before other things?

20. How did God:
    A. Prepare Elizabeth for Mary's visit?

    B. Give Elizabeth support through Mary?

    C. Give Elizabeth support through friends and relatives?

21. What are some of the greatest needs in your life right now? What could you learn from this lesson that is helpful in regard to your needs?

22. If time permits, share one thing God has impressed on you from this lesson. (Give women the freedom to pass.)

Prayer Time

Many people are intimidated by the idea of praying out loud. This guide will gently lead you into this gradually. And no one will ever be forced to pray out loud.

Elizabeth encouraged Mary by affirming her faith, by blessing her. Today, stand in a circle holding hands. Each woman will bless the woman on her right in prayer. She might say something like: "Thank You for Cindy—for her gentleness." If she doesn't know Cindy, she can say, "Lord, bless Cindy." If she doesn't want to speak out loud, she can bless Cindy silently and squeeze Cindy's hand. Then Cindy will bless the woman on her right.

Second Stop!
Mary Found Favor

*H*ow many sermons have you heard about Mary? Evangelicals and Protestants tend to neglect her, TO OUR GREAT LOSS! She, alone among women, was chosen to be the mother of the Messiah.

Gabriel tells Mary she has found favor (*charis*) or grace, with God. Dr. Darrell L. Bock explains that "favor signifies God's gracious choice of someone through whom God does something special (Noah is spared from the Flood; Gideon is chosen to judge Israel; Hannah is given a child in barrenness . . .)."[1]

Can we do something to receive favor from God? Scripture is clear that our righteousness is pitiful when compared to a Holy God (Isaiah 64:6). If there is anything good in us, it comes through faith in God. As you look at Noah, Abraham, Hannah, and Mary, you will find one common quality—faith. In Luke's Gospel you will repeatedly see that it is faith that pleases Jesus. For example, Jesus commends the bleeding woman who touched His cloak, saying, "Daughter, your faith has healed you. Go in peace" (Luke 8:48). Likewise, Mary demonstrates faith when her immediate response, in sharp contrast to Zechariah's, is faith. And Elizabeth, when prophesying through the power of the Spirit, says to Mary: "Blessed is she who has believed that what the Lord has said to her will be accomplished!" (Luke 1:45)

What would happen in your life if you trusted God as Mary did?

Prepare Your Heart to Hear

Before each of the following six devotional times, quiet your heart and ask God to speak to you personally from His Word. Then, like Mary, trust that He will!

Memory Work
Add Luke 1:48 to Luke 1:46-47.

> **And Mary said: "My soul praises the Lord and my spirit rejoices in God my Savior, For He has been mindful of the humble state of His servant. From now on all generations will call me blessed."**

Warm-Up
Artists throughout the centuries have tried to capture this incredible moment of the "Annunciation." If you could paint it, how would you portray Mary's face? Gabriel? The light? The surroundings?

Day 1: Overview
1. Read over the introductory notes for THE SECOND STOP! MARY FOUND FAVOR (p. 22). What stood out to you?

As an overview, read Luke 1:26-56.

Spend five minutes on the memory passage.

Day 2: Mary Found Favor with God
In some liturgical churches, the "Annunciation" is celebrated on the 25th of March. "Annunciation" means "to announce, to bring tidings." Gabriel announced to Mary that she would be "overshadowed by the Holy Spirit" to conceive Jesus. John 1 makes it clear this was not the beginning of Jesus' life, but simply the beginning of His time in the flesh. The Word made flesh. A paradox poets have pondered. John Donne calls it "immensity cloistered in a womb." Luci Shaw describes the enigma as: "the Word, stern sentenced to be nine months dumb."

Read Luke 1:26-38.

2.   Try to get to know Mary through the following verses. List anything you discover *or discern* about her.

    A. Luke 1:26-28

    B. Luke 1:29

    C. Luke 1:30-33

    D. Luke 1:34

    E. Luke 1:35-37

    F. Luke 1:38

    G. Luke 1:39

3.   What would your life be like today if you, like Mary, were to live a completely yielded life? Consider any areas you have held back.

4. Scripture tells us the following people (among others) found favor in His eyes or that He granted them favor in the eyes of others. Explain how they demonstrated faith and also how they found favor.

    A. Noah (Genesis 6, particularly verses 8-9 and 22)

    B. Joseph (Genesis 39, particularly verses 2-10 and 21)

    C. Hannah (1 Samuel 1–2, particularly 1:9-20 and 2:1-10)

    D. Abraham (Romans 4:13-22)

5. How can we increase our faith according to the following?

    A. Romans 10:17

    B. Mark 9:24

    C. Luke 17:5

    D. James 2:20-22

Poet Luci Shaw says that Mary asks Gabriel to widen her imagination.[2] *In effect, she says, "I believe You are going to do this, Lord—but, I am a virgin, so how?"*

In your personal quiet time, ask God to show you where you are not trusting Him. Ask Him to strengthen your faith, to "widen your imagination" in what He is able to do. Then be alert to be amazed.

Review the memory passage.

Day 3: Mary, Stepping Out on Faith

Mary was responsive to God, realizing Gabriel has mentioned Elizabeth for a reason. On faith, she makes the long journey to Elizabeth's home. There, God will increase her faith through Elizabeth's pregnancy, prophecy, and life.

6.   Review the last lesson on Elizabeth and list some of the things Elizabeth had learned which might be valuable in Mary's future.

7.   Look at a Bible map and estimate how far Mary walked in order to visit Elizabeth. (Mary lived in Nazareth and Elizabeth in the hill country outside of Jerusalem.) To put yourself in Mary's shoes, name a destination from your home of similar distance. (If there is a route that goes through hilly country, choose it!)
    Those who walked covered about twenty miles a day. How long did this take Mary?

    Considering the length and difficulty of this trip, why do you think Mary went?

8. How sensitive are you to the leading of the Holy Spirit in friendship?
   A. When God brings someone to mind, or across your path, are you alert to how God would have you respond?

   B. When facing a difficult situation, do you consider a godly older woman who has been where you are going and done it well? Or do you automatically run to a peer?

   C. Share a time when you were blessed by being sensitive to the Holy Spirit in friendship.

Day 4: The Greeting Scene

In *The Book of God: The Bible as a Novel*, Walter Wangerin, Jr. imagines the following thoughts and feelings in Mary and Elizabeth during their amazing greeting scene:

Zechariah didn't hear the knock. Zechariah wouldn't have heard a hammer on his anvil or thunder in the heavens. Ever since the night of his "vision of angels," as he described it in writing for her—the old nailsmith had been completely deaf and dumb.

So Elizabeth opened her door herself—and there stood her nephew's child, Joachim's little girl, whom she had not seen in years. "Mary!" Elizabeth cried. "Pretty Mary, it's you! But you're alone!"

But this was no common visit.

And Mary was not a child anymore.

Her dark brows were lifted in an intense appeal, and her eyes were filled with beseeching. Clearly, she had come with a question.

Then several things happened so swiftly that they were all one thing, and that thing was the revelation of God.

Mary's eyes dropped to Elizabeth's breasts and then to her belly. In the softest of whispers, she said, "Hail, Elizabeth."

Immediately the baby in Elizabeth's womb leaped up to her heart, and old Elizabeth shrieked.

Because Elizabeth suddenly understood everything: the child inside of her, the reason for Mary's appearing, the glory of the days in which they were living, the great thing that God was starting to do!

"Oh, Mary!" Elizabeth cried. She grabbed her young niece by both her arms and pulled her into the house. "Mary, blessed are you among women, and blessed is the fruit of your womb!"

Mary mouthed the words, My womb?[3]

9.   Comment on Wangerin's description. What thoughts do *you* think were going on in each woman?

10.   Go through Elizabeth's greeting and imagine how each of the following verses impacted Mary:
    A. Luke 1:42

    B. Luke 1:43

C. Luke 1:44

D. Luke 1:45

11. Share a time when you trusted God and God showed you favor.

Review the memory passage.

Day 5: Mary's Magnificat

This famous "Virgin's Hymn" has been used in public liturgies over the centuries. Contemporary praise choruses likewise draw upon Mary's ponderings. Mark Lowry wrote: "Mary, did you know that the One you delivered will soon deliver you?" I believe her Magnificat shows that, yes, she at least understood dimly. Her soul rejoices in God her *Savior*. She seems to know many things, evidencing that she was very familiar with the Psalms, with Hannah's song, and Scripture in general. Her Magnificat is also a beautiful demonstration of the anointing of the Spirit on this woman who found favor with God.

Read Luke 1:46-55.

12. Meditate on the Magnificat.
    A. Luke 1:46-49—Mary praises God for being personal. What are some of the thoughts which overwhelm her?

    B. Mary's words echo the psalmist's words. How do you see this in Psalm 8:3-5? In Psalm 138:6?

    C. How is Mary's song similar to Hannah's song? (1 Samuel 2)

D. Based on her Magnificat, do you think Mary expected a suffering Savior? Explain.

13. What impresses you most from the Magnificat?

Personal Action Assignment

Write your own song of praise. (Include ways God has been mindful of you, ways you have seen His power and mercy in your life, or in the lives of those from past generations.)

Close by reflectively singing "Joy to the World" which is actually a song about the second coming of Christ.

Day 6: Mary Stayed Three Months

We are left to imagine what happened during those three months, for Luke does not supply us with those details. Some of the things that I imagine, from my perspective as a woman, are some valuable mentoring time with Elizabeth where Mary watched her and learned how to be a godly wife. I believe they talked about how to raise boys, made blue layettes together, and helped each other find strength in God through prayer, through praise, and through sharing what they knew about prophecy.

Recently I was visiting with a woman who said: "My friends are believers—but all they talk about is their kids and their activities. They don't talk about the Lord or their need for support in overcoming their sinful tendencies. I long for a deeper kind of friendship." Surely Mary and Elizabeth had this in each other. Jesus says that our words reflect the overflow of our hearts. Because Elizabeth and Mary spent so much time alone with the Lord, their words became a fountain of strength to one another. Perhaps Elizabeth shared with Mary some of the things God taught her during her long time of barrenness. There were going to be many times in Mary's future when life would be difficult. I imagine that Elizabeth's words came back to her, helping her to face the difficulties of life with trust that God was good and would do all things well in His time.

I also believe that Mary was there when John the Baptist was born even though Luke does not say she was there. (But there are many things we are not told!) We know Elizabeth was a little more than six months pregnant when Mary arrived—and we know Mary stayed three months. It makes sense to me as a woman that Mary stayed three months in order to help Elizabeth with the birth and the new baby. I think that is precisely why Mary stayed so long! Mary didn't know that in six months she would be giving birth on a bare barn floor without mother or midwife. But God knew. God knew Mary's needs better than she did. I believe He provided her with the valuable mentoring experience of seeing a baby being born, of seeing the umbilical cord tied and cut, of seeing that baby washed and wrapped in swaddling clothes—because He loved Mary, and He wanted to prepare her.

> *The assertion of Luke that Mary returned home (verse 56) does not necessarily imply that she did not wait for John's birth and circumcision. The probabilities are in favour of supposing that she did so wait, and received the additional consolations which the song of Zacharias was so able to bring back.*
>
> *R.M. Edgar in* The Pulpit Commentary[4]

14. What do you imagine happened during the three months Mary spent with Elizabeth? Why?

15. If Mary talked to Joseph before she left, she probably knew that he did not believe her story. How might have Elizabeth provided comfort and strength through her experience?

If you are married, have there been godly older women in your life who have helped you to be a better wife or to give your husband some grace? If so, what did they say or do?

16. Do you have friends who encourage you spiritually when you are with them, as Mary and Elizabeth encouraged each other? If so, what is it about their conversations that strengthens you?

17. Do you think you are an encouragement spiritually to others through your conversation? If so, how? If not, what changes could you make so you are an encouragement?

Prayer Time

One of the best ways to encourage one another spiritually is through prayer. In order to pray effectively for one another, it is important to be honest and vulnerable with one another. Have each woman write down a need in her life on an index card. She can sign the card or leave it unsigned. Then place the cards face down in the center. Each woman should draw a card out and commit to praying for that need all week. (The group needs to commit now to keeping confidences within the group.) In the prayer time next week, give the women an opportunity to share if the needs they wrote on their cards were met.

Third Stop!
Detectives for the Divine

Mary was a ponderer. Repeatedly we are told "she pondered, or she treasured these things in her heart." *Often the difference between someone who lives a wasted life and someone who lives a fruitful life is that they choose to reflect on the things of God* (Luke 10:42; Psalm 1). In this hurried life, reflective souls are rare—yet we are commanded to "live quiet lives" (1 Timothy 2:2). Is that possible in a day of carpooling, cable television, and church meeting mania?

Yes. Some succeed in choosing the reflective life. They say no to outside voices and carve out reflective times. They do their Bible study thoughtfully, making notes, asking God to speak to them. They keep journals, they read, and they are constantly looking at life like detectives for the Divine.

Will the next generation have individuals who are ponderers? Yes, God has always had a remnant, people like Mary, Simeon, and Anna who seek Him. Many have been trained to seek Him, having had mothers who guarded them from too much television and too many outside activities. These mothers knew that reflective souls need time to read, to converse, and to be outdoors in God's creation.

Prepare Your Heart to Hear
Before each of the following six devotional times, quiet your heart and ask God to speak to you personally from His Word.

Memory Work
Complete Luke 1:46-50.

And Mary said: "My soul praises the Lord and my spirit rejoices in God my Savior, For He has been mindful of the humble state of His servant. From now on all generations will call me blessed, for the Mighty One has done great things for Me—holy is His name. His mercy extends to those who fear Him, from generation to generation."

Warm-Up

Ponder why some women are wonderful detectives for the Divine and others, though believers, miss His voice, His wonder, His deep revelations, and His paths on a daily basis. List everything that might make the difference.

Day 1: Overview

1.   Read over the introductory notes for THE THIRD STOP! DETECTIVES FOR THE DIVINE (p. 33) along with the Scriptures. What stood out to you?

2.   Do you think you (and your family) live quiet, reflective lives? If so, what do you do? If not, what might you do differently?

Personal Action Assignment

Share with your husband what you have been learning about the importance of quiet, reflective time and consider how you are doing as a family. Is the Lord leading you to make any changes? If so, what?

Meditate on Luke 2:19, 51.

Learn the memory passage.

Day 2: Reflecting on Scripture

Reflective people look at Scripture with fresh eyes, trying to get in the place of the historical people, never forgetting that these were real people. They also learn to ask questions like the questions of a detective:

Where did this happen? (and is that significant?)
What happened?
Why did it happen?
Who was involved?
How did they feel?

Imagine that you and Joseph have just reached the crest of Bethlehem. You look at the terraced vineyards, the fields of wheat, the hillsides dotted with sheep. You imagine Ruth gleaning in the fields and David as a young shepherd boy. From this little town God raised up rulers and you know He is about to do it again—for you are great with the Savior. For nine months you have pondered what Gabriel said to you. For nine months you have been examining the prophecies concerning the Messiah. One you recall is from the Prophet Micah, recorded nearly 700 years before.

But you, Bethlehem Ephrathah,
though you are small among the clans of Judah,
out of you will come for Me
one who will be ruler over Israel,
whose origins are from of old,
from ancient times.

Micah 5:2

3. Do you have a special place on earth that floods your heart with memories, or is precious to you because of its history? If so, what thoughts and feelings come to you when you visit it?

4. What are some things that have happened in Bethlehem?
   A. Genesis 35:19

B. Ruth 1:16-22

C. Ruth 4:11-22

D. 1 Samuel 16:1-13

E. Matthew 1:5-6, 16

5. Why do you think God chose Bethlehem for the Savior's birthplace?

Do you see any significance that Rachel, or Ruth, or David were linked to Bethlehem? (Choose one and use your imagination.)

6. Write down some of the thoughts Mary might have been having as she overlooked Bethlehem. (Take time. Ask the questions: Why, how, where, and what was she feeling?)

Review your memory passage.

Day 3: The Shepherds

Often those who work alone outdoors (like shepherds and farmers) have developed a spiritual sensitivity. It is difficult (though not impossible) to consider the heavens and not think of God, or to observe the change of seasons and not think of the Creator. Often those who work outdoors become detectives for the Divine, seeing God's hand in the instinct of the bumblebee or the falling leaves which fertilize the soil.

Fruitful believers are aware of God's sovereignty, that He brings events and people into our lives for a reason. When the shepherds visited Mary, "she treasured up all of these things and pondered them in her heart" (Luke 2:19).

Read Luke 2:8-15. Use a paraphrase or fresh translation.

7.   Have you found that being outdoors alone stimulates your thoughts of God? If so, share something about it.

8.   Imagine you are a shepherd. What might your life be like?

Note:
Historical records indicate these shepherds may have raised lambs for the temple sacrifice, giving them increased spiritual awareness.

9.   Imagine you experienced what the shepherds experienced that night. How might you feel? What might you tell others?

Reflect on the woodcut on page 9 by Gustave Dore. What does the artist communicate to you?

Read Luke 2:16-19. Review the memory passage (Luke 2:19).

10. The shepherds have left. Pretend you are Mary, journaling, recording evidences for the reality of God in your life. What are some possible entries you might make in your journal?

11. Move back into your own shoes. What evidence for the reality of God in your life might you record from the last few months?

12. Why is it wise to record these things, to keep them in your "treasure chest"? If you are not in the habit of doing this, what small step might you make toward beginning?

I keep a journal in which I record times I have spied God in my life. One of the times God was particularly near to me was when my husband was planning to leave me—and when he did. Again and again God reached out through the love of friends, through the ways He was so obviously trying to get my husband's attention, and through His presence, so unmistakingly real, so strong. . . . Now, when the road is lonely and I question, "Was God really with me? Or was it my imagination?" I look back and see, in black and white, that, yes, He was with me.

Peg, as told in The Friendships of Women[5]

Day 4: Simeon

Seldom have I had a personal prophecy given to me, but I will never forget the first. When I had just begun my speaking ministry, shortly after the release of *The Friendships of Women,* a shy young woman approached me after I spoke, saying she had a message from the Lord for me. She said she was frightened, but the Lord had made it clear that she was to give me a message. Then, with trembling hands, she pulled out a tape recorder and recorded what she told me, which was about three minutes of prophecy concerning my future ministry. In beautiful poetry she talked about how God was anointing me to restore mothers and daughters; mothers-in-law and daughters-in-law; friends; sisters; and sisters in Christ. Though she had not known I was going to speak about Ruth and Naomi that night, her prophecy was laced with their names and the names of those I would speak about in the future: Mary, Elizabeth, Rachel, and Leah.

At the time I marveled—and I wondered if it could be true. Now, ten years later, I marvel even more—for that has been exactly how God has anointed me over these last ten years.

In Luke alone we read of the prophecy Simeon gave to Mary.

Comment on the above.

13. Have you had an experience of God speaking to you through a prophecy or exhortation in His Word, or through His still small voice? If so, share briefly.

Read Luke 2:21-35.

14. What evidence do you find for Simeon being a reflective person? How was he rewarded?

Simeon attained the desire of his heart, to see the Messiah. God allowed him to recognize the Messiah in Mary's arms. "It is right for those who are taking a very earnest interest in the cause of Christ to long to be allowed to accomplish a certain work for him."

W. Clarkson, The Pulpit Commentary[6]

15. Do you long to accomplish a particular work for Christ? If so, what is it?

16. Here at the birth, only Simeon seems to have grasped the titanic struggle that will follow this baby. List at least four things which the Holy Spirit revealed to Simeon (Luke 2:34-35).

17. Later, after the Crucifixion and Resurrection, the Holy Spirit gave understanding to other disciples about the spiritual warfare surrounding Jesus.
   A. What did God reveal to Peter about this? (1 Peter 2:7-8)

   B. What did God reveal to John about this? (Revelation 12:1-5)

Philip Yancey says he has never seen the above verse from Revelation on a Christmas card. "In daily life two parallel histories occur simultaneously, one on earth and one in heaven. Revelation, however, views them together, allowing a quick look behind the scenes. On earth a baby was born, a king got wind of it, a chase ensued. In heaven the Great Invasion had begun, a daring raid by the ruler of the forces of good into the universe's seat of evil."[7]

18. Tristine Rainier writes: "An experienced diarist . . . is willing to place questions in the diary and wait for answers." Put yourself in Mary's place as she listens to Simeon's prophecy. Write down some questions she might have placed in her diary.

At the end of her life, what might have been some of the answers to those questions?

Like Mary, we will experience sorrow in life for Jesus told us life is filled with trouble (John 16:33). And, if we are living godly lives, we will experience the same kind of spiritual battle that surrounded Jesus (2 Timothy 3:12).

19. Wise believers record questions in their journals concerning the sorrow they are experiencing or have experienced and then wait for the answers. What questions might you record?

Day 5: Anna

Anna was a widow for most of her life. One of the advantages of singleness for a believer is that she is more apt to learn to be truly dependent on God and to find that He indeed is sufficient (1 Corinthians 7:25-40; 1 Timothy 5:5). Amy Carmichael, the single missionary to India, whose journals have inspired so many, tells of the struggle she had in her youth as God asked her: "Am I not enough, My own—not enough for you?" Amy writes:

It was a long time before I could honestly answer, "Yes, You alone are enough for me." I remember the turmoil of soul I experienced before committing myself to follow Him on whatever path He would lead— remember as if it were yesterday. But at last—oh, the rest that came to me when I lifted my head and followed! For in acceptance there lies peace.
                    Amy Carmichael, Candles in the Dark[8]

Read Luke 2:36-38.

20. Put yourself in Anna's shoes. Imagine her life, her feelings.

What evidence do you find for Anna being a reflective person? How was she rewarded?

21. Have you discovered that God alone is enough for you—or are you still in the process of learning that?

22. Are you in the habit of spending time alone with God in Scripture and in prayer on a daily basis? If so, share when, where, and how you go about this.

Day 6: Mary Treasured These Things in Her Heart

As in Luke 2:19, after the shepherd's visit, here again, in Luke 2:51, after listening to the amazing words of her twelve-year-old son, we are told: "His mother treasured all these things in her heart."

In a charming fictional book called *Mary's Journal,* Evelyn Bence says that while she knows that women of that day did not read or write, they did memorize God's Word and keep it in their hearts. And because Mary is repeatedly called a "ponderer," Evelyn says that "she is the kind of woman who, if alive today, would keep a journal."

Chuck Swindoll says: "Thoughts untangle themselves as they go down from the lips and through the fingertips." In my journal I record what God teaches me through His Word—and that helps me to be alert to His still small voice. I record my prayers and, subsequently, I highlight the answers to those prayers.

Your personal action assignment is to purchase a journal. I prefer a spiralbound journal with a hardcover, though a good stiff cardboard cover will do.

Read Luke 2:41-52.

Evelyn Bence helps us to get in Mary's shoes, imagining the prayers and questions she might have recorded in her journal during this time:

> Heaven be merciful. Jesus is gone. We've canvassed the whole caravan and no one has seen him since we broke up camp this morning. All day I've thought him with Joseph and the men . . . Joseph assumed he, still a child after all, was with me and the women. . . .
>
> Guilt: my utter lack of responsibility. I, given such a privileged charge, have let him—still a boy—slip out of my shelter. Will I find forgiveness for such gross negligence?
>
> . . . "Didn't you know I'd be here tending my Father's affairs?"
> Wait, go back to the angel's announcement of this coming child: "He will be called the Son of the Most High." . . . Was Jesus saying something important to me?
>
> Evelyn Bence, Mary's Journal[9]

23. Have you ever lost a child who was in your care? If so, what did you feel?

Gleaning from this passage, what phrases help you to know what Mary might have been feeling?

What questions do you imagine she might have put in her journal after this episode?

Extra Credit
Read Luke 3–6.

Personal Action Assignment
Purchase a journal today!

Review your memory verse.

Prayer Time
Give women an opportunity to share if the prayer they recorded on the card last week was met.

Then ask for specific prayer requests and pray conversationally. The following diagram explains "popcorn prayer."

Popcorn Prayer

Close with the chorus from "O Come All Ye Faithful" (O Come Let Us Adore Him).

the
Second Oasis

THE SAVIOR'S POWER

A squall came down on the lake, so that
the boat was being swamped, and they
were in great danger.
—Luke 8:23

the Second Oasis

The Savior's Power
(Luke 7–9)

He wasn't what they expected. He didn't hurl lightning bolts or float about the sky on a throne. Even John the Baptist, imprisoned, seems confused. He sent his disciples to Jesus to ask: "Are You the one who was to come, or should we expect someone else?" (Luke 7:20)

Philip Yancey *(The Jesus I Never Knew)* says that the Gospels read "like a 'Whodunit' (or as Alister McGrath has pointed out, a 'whowashe') detective story."[10] In Luke 7–9, the crowds keep asking: "Who is He?" He's obviously a V.I.P.—but who? When He heals a Gentile's servant, it seems He is a prophet. Then, when He raises a widow's only begotten son (told only in Luke), the people surmise He is in the *upper echelon* of prophets, like Elijah or Elisha, who also raised the dead. When Jesus forgives the sins of a repentant woman at the house of Simon, they ask: "Who is this who even forgives sins?" (Luke 7:49) When He stops the storm, the disciples say: "Who is this? He commands even the winds and the water, and they obey Him" (Luke 8:25).

Who is He? A prophet? A great prophet? The Messiah? God Himself? In this oasis, you will see the majesty of His birth repeated in the majesty of His miracles. All this is leading to the climax of Luke, which is Peter's confession when Jesus asks him, "Who do you say I am?"

Peter answers: "The Christ of God" (Luke 9:20).

Fourth Stop!
Who Is This Who Even Forgives Sins?

significant theme in Luke is the universality of Christ's promises. All questions of social class, race, and gender break down. For example, Luke *alone* tells us about:

The shepherds (CHRIST CAME FOR THE POOR!)

The Good Samaritan (CHRIST CAME FOR THE OUTSIDER!)

Elizabeth, Anna, the grieving widow, Mary of Bethany sitting at His feet . . . (CHRIST CAME FOR WOMEN!)

The religions of men discriminate against women. Many orthodox Jewish males prayed daily: "Thank You God I was not born a woman." But Jesus elevated women, obliterating worldly divisions. When the Pharisees shun the sinful woman who pours perfume on Jesus, Jesus rebukes their self-righteousness and asks, instead: "Will you come to Me in humble faith as this woman has?" If we do, Jesus tells us clearly, we are part of His family. The issue is not gender, nor class, nor race—but faith and obedience! "My mother and brothers are those who hear God's word and put it into practice" (Luke 8:21).

Prepare Your Heart to Hear
Before each of the following six devotional times, remember that it is not familiarity but obedience to God's truth that pleases Him.

Memory Work
Review your memory work from The First Oasis.
Then, for The Second Oasis, you will be memorizing Luke 9:23-25. Begin this week with verse 23.

Then He said to them all: "If anyone would come after Me, he must deny himself and take up his cross daily and follow Me."

Warm-Up

The crowds couldn't help but be amazed by Jesus. He was different—He responded to the faith of Gentiles and women! His miracles caused crowds to follow Him. But soon they discovered His teachings were hard, the cost of discipleship high. Offended, they began to fall away. In the climax of chapter 7, Jesus says: "Blessed is he who is not offended because of Me" (v. 23, NKJV). Name a teaching of our Lord which offends the world or which you struggle to completely obey.

Day 1: Overview

1. Read all of the introductory notes. Comment on what stood out to you from:
    A. The Introductory notes for THE SECOND OASIS: THE SAVIOR'S POWER (p. 46)

    B. The Introductory notes for THE FOURTH STOP! WHO IS THIS WHO EVEN FORGIVES SINS? (p. 47)

Read Luke 7 as an overview. Watch for the escalating mystery concerning the identity of Jesus.

Spend five minutes on the memory passages.

Journal Entry: Spend three minutes entering a few remarks in your journal on what God impressed on your heart.

Day 2: He Responds to Outsiders!

Sometimes I am amazed when I meet a spiritual giant and then discover he did not have the advantage of a Christian home. I think that is the way Jesus felt when He met the centurion, a Gentile whose faith surpassed the faith of His own Jewish disciples. The centurion had not witnessed the miracles of Jesus firsthand, nor did he ask to touch Jesus. Instead, he sent two delegations to Jesus, asking Jesus to heal his beloved slave from a distance. A man of power who commanded thousands in the Roman army, the centurion was still a humble man, saying he was unworthy to have Jesus come to his house. The Jews respected him, saying he had built their synagogue. (The ruins of a white marble synagogue still stand in Capernaum.) The centurion's military mind uses an army analogy, saying that Jesus had authority over thousands of angels!

Read Luke 7:1-10.

2.   Find many evidences that the centurion was a man of character and of faith.

3.   What differences do you see between the faith of Simon Peter and that of the centurion in the following passages:
   A. Luke 4:38

   B. Matthew 26:50-53 (John tells us it was Peter who cut off the soldier's ear. Luke tells us Jesus healed the soldier.)

4.   What similarity do you see between Simon Peter and the centurion in Luke 5:5-8?

Have you ever experienced an intense feeling of unworthiness after a particular act of goodness from God? If so, share.

5.   Though the centurion was an outsider, a Gentile, a man of a different race, Jesus responded to him and commended his faith. This is a central message in Luke, one which he heard Paul proclaim repeatedly as he traveled with him. How do the following teachings of Paul explain or elaborate on the universality of Christ's promises to those who believe?
   A. Galatians 3:7-9

   B. Galatians 3:28-29

   C. Ephesians 2:8-20

6.   Satan longs for us to be divided in our homes, in our churches, and in the body of Christ. He wants us to be prejudiced, to judge each other on the basis of race, class, gender, or denomination! One of the beautiful aspects of the story of the centurion was to see how the Jews and Gentiles loved and respected each other as they shared faith in God. What do you learn from the following passages about the importance of love and unity?
   A. 1 Corinthians 1:1-13

   B. 1 Corinthians 3:3-9

C. John 17:20-23

In John 17:20-23, Jesus' last prayer before the cross was for us, that we as believers would love each other. Why? So that the world will believe Christianity is true.

> We cannot expect the world to believe that the Father sent the Son, that Jesus' claims are true, and that Christianity is true, unless the world sees some reality of the oneness of true Christians.
>   Francis Schaeffer, The Church at the End of the Twentieth Century[11]

Review your memory work.

Personal Action Assignment
7. Are you aware of any division between you and a member of the body of Christ? What could you do to increase peace between you?

8. Do you, like the centurion, believe that Jesus can intervene and answer prayer? If so, come to Him now in fervent Intercessory prayer. Record your requests here or in your journal.

Day 3: He Must Be in the Upper Echelon of Prophets!
Now we move to another "woman's story" told only in Luke. Jesus amazes the crowd by stopping a funeral procession. Moved with compassion by seeing the "only son" of a widow carried out, Jesus touches the dead man and commands him, as He did with Lazarus, to rise! Abruptly the son sat up and "Jesus gave him

back to his mother." The crowd is "seized with fear" and reassesses their opinion of Jesus. The only prophets who have raised the dead were the cream of the cream: Elijah and Elisha. Jesus is not only a prophet—He is a "great prophet!"

9. Meditate on Luke 7:11-17 and then answer:
    A. Even the word "widow" has a connotation of sorrow. If you are a widow, share something of the sorrow of widowhood. If you are not, try to imagine what would be some of the things you would miss.

    B. What hope and comfort would a son who had reached young manhood provide?

    C. What phrase describes the motive for this healing?

Personal Reflection Only

Is there a heartache or concern in your life which you have been carrying alone? Sing "Turn Your Eyes Upon Jesus" from your hymnal. As you sing, put your burden in the strong arms of Jesus.

10. How, according to 1 John 3:14-18, should our response be like that of Jesus in this account? Why?

Personal Action Assignment

Ask the Lord to open your eyes and to give you compassion for someone in need in your life. Then ask the Lord to show you a specific way to respond and do it. (You will tell one person in the group next week what you did.)

Review your memory verse.

11. What is the response of the crowd to the raising of this young man from the dead?

Why do you think fear often follows miracles in the New Testament? How do you think you would feel if the raising of the young man happened today?

Day 4: But Is He the Messiah?

In this key section, John the Baptist, who has been imprisoned for confronting Herod about his adulterous affair, sends his disciples to Jesus to ask: "Are You the one who was to come, or should we expect someone else?" (Luke 7:19)

Doesn't John know Jesus is the Messiah? Is John using the Socratic method, asking a question so that Jesus can clarify to the crowds who He is? Possibly, though it would be understandable if John himself had questions. He is in prison for doing what was right and Jesus is not miraculously releasing him. Why not? Is Jesus truly the Messiah?

Jesus answers John by showing that He has been fulfilling Isaiah's prophecies concerning the Messiah. And then Jesus gives a gentle rebuke: "And blessed is he, whosoever shall not be offended in Me" (Luke 7:23, KJV).

We need to take these words to heart. The words of Jesus are still offending people—and even believers have trouble trusting wholeheartedly. Jesus asks us to put Him first in our lives, even over our devotion to husbands, children, and parents (Luke 14:26). He asks us to look for reward in the spiritual rather than the material (Matthew 5:29). He asks us to deny ourselves, to lose ourselves completely in Him! (Luke 9:23) These are hard sayings, but Jesus says that if we are not offended by them, but instead embrace them wholly, we will be greatly blessed.

Certainly many secular women today are offended by the idea that women should wait until marriage for sexual intimacy, should be in submission to their husbands, and should stay married for life. Likewise, people scoff at the idea of hell, yet Jesus teaches clearly about it (Luke 12:5). The reason God sent Jesus to die on a cross was to pay the price for our sin and to save anyone who would believe from the fires of hell. The message of the cross is foolishness to those who are perishing (1 Corinthians 1:18).

How do you respond to Jesus? If you believe that He is, indeed, the Messiah, then will you embrace and obey His radical teachings? If you do, you will indeed be blessed!

Review your memory passage.

Read Luke 7:18-23.

12. How does Jesus respond to John the Baptist's question?

13. Explain how His response shows a fulfillment of messianic prophecy:
A. Isaiah 26:19

B. Isaiah 29:18-19

C. Isaiah 35:5-6

D. Isaiah 61:1

14. Jesus continues in Luke with hard teachings. Summarize the hard teaching in each of the following passages and then answer: "How am I truly responding to this teaching?"
A. Luke 9:23-25

B. Luke 12:4-5

C. Luke 12:15

D. Luke 12:27-31

Read Luke 7:27-35.

15. How does Jesus commend the character of John the Baptist in verse 28?

16. What have you seen in John the Baptist that was worthy of praise? (See Luke 3:7-9, 15-16, 19.)

17. Jesus then condemns the Pharisees who were offended by John and now by Jesus. They claimed to be offended by the lifestyle of both of them, but in reality, they were offended by the hard message of repentance and faith. How does Jesus show this in verses 31-35?

When Jesus compares the people to children in 7:31-32, He is saying: Unless you can make the rules to the game, you don't want to play. To many it seems more attractive to make up their own religion than to follow the hard teachings of Jesus.

Personal Action Assignment

Are you offended by Jesus' hard sayings? If not, but instead desire to embrace Him wholeheartedly, how should you live today? Be still before the Lord. Journal what He impresses on your heart. Then *walk* in the Spirit!

Day 5: Who But God Can Forgive Sins?

Imagine the scene. A dinner party at a fine home. A woman with an immoral past shocks the guests by entering, falling on her knees before Jesus, and pouring an expensive jar of perfume on His feet. Then, adding one shock to another, this "prophet" tells her that her sins are forgiven! The nerve! Who does this man think He is? After all, who has the authority to forgive sins but God alone? (This incident, another "woman's incident," is found only in Luke. Many do not realize this, confusing this incident with a different incident involving the devout Mary of Bethany which we will study in The Third Oasis.)

The message in this incident is that repentance and faith are necessary for salvation. In fact, that is all that is necessary! Dr. Darrell Bock told me: "There is a marvelous lesson here for those with a lurid past. This message of forgiveness for *anyone* is Luke's emphasis." The Pharisees reject this message, and attack the messenger (Luke 7:33-35). So Jesus then turns to His host, Simon the Pharisee, and says, in words that would have stopped my heart, "Simon, I have something to tell you" (Luke 7:40).

Read Luke 7:36-50.

18. Contrast the heart of Simon with the heart of the sinful woman. Give Scripture references to support your answer.

The woman   *Simon the Pharisee*

19. How does Jesus help Simon to understand the difference between his heart and the heart of the woman?

Day 6: Have You Ever Wept for Your Sins?

At the age of twenty-one I was confronted with the claims of Christ. The more I examined Jesus, much as the people are doing in Luke 7, the more in awe I grew. Could it be? Could this Man who came to earth actually be God? Was His death on the cross a purposeful choice to pay for my sin? And when He said that He was the only way to heaven, was He telling the truth?

I remember the November day I fell on my knees and surrendered my life to Christ. At that moment, God's Holy Spirit opened my eyes to three things, in rapid succession:

1. The profound holiness of God
2. My own wretched sinfulness
3. God's amazing grace in washing me of my sin

And I, like this sinful woman in Luke 7, wept in gratitude. Then, more than anything, I wanted to live fully for Christ! If you have never wept for your sin, if you have never been overwhelmed with gratitude toward Jesus, perhaps you have yet to realize who Jesus is and what He did for you.

20. Has there ever been a time when you, like the sinful woman in Luke, wept for your sin? If so, share something about your feelings at the time.

Have there also been times when, like Simon the Pharisee, you lacked gratitude and an awareness of all Jesus is and is giving you? If so, how can you increase your thankfulness?

Sing "Amazing Grace" in your personal devotional time as a way of praising God.

21. What evidence is there in your life that you are profoundly thankful to Jesus?

Read Luke 8:1-3.

22. What do you learn about the women who traveled with Jesus?

These women had experienced the power of Jesus in their lives and now were helping to support Him. It is likely that they were one of Luke's sources of information. Dr. Darrell Bock tells us the following about them:

An itinerant ministry like Jesus' was common, and support from women was common; but it was unusual for women to travel with a rabbi. The first woman, Mary Magdalene, was freed from the presence of seven demons. . . . she was not the sinful woman who anointed Jesus. Nor is it clear that she was immoral. . . . Mary stayed faithful to Jesus, for it is recorded that she watched the Crucifixion, saw where Jesus was laid, and participated in the anointing of the body. . . . The mention of Joanna who also is present with Mary Magdalene in Luke 24:10, indicates the scope of Jesus' ministry. Jesus, message had reached into the world of the powerful, for Joanna was the wife of Chuza, who served as an administrative official in Herod's court. . . . The third woman, Susanna, is mentioned only here. . . .[12]

23. If time permits, have women share the lesson God impressed on their hearts through this study.

Prayer Time

Instead of sharing individual prayer requests, have each woman lift her own request up in prayer. Then have a few women support her with sentences. When there is a silence, another woman should lift up her individual prayer request. Close with a familiar chorus such as "God Is So Good."

Fifth Stop!
Who Is This Who Stops Storms?

C he disciples have seen Jesus do miracles that only the greatest of prophets have done. Recently they saw Him claim to forgive sins. Their minds are swirling.

Now two things happen that escalate the drama. Up to now the miracles of Jesus have impacted others. Now they themselves are the recipients. Also, up to now the miracles of Jesus had also been performed by the greatest of prophets. Now He does something that has never been done. He stops a raging storm on the sea. Imagine the scene.

Fishermen say the storms on the Sea of Galilee are formidable. With Jesus asleep in the boat, the disciples are overcome by fear as lightning crashes next to them and waves swamp the boat. They cry out to Jesus in terror. I am not sure what they expected Him to do, but what He does do astonishes them. He stands and rebukes the wind and the raging waters. Immediately all was calm. The disciples look at one another in fear—for now they feared the POWER of the One who stopped the storm even more than the storm. "Who is this? He commands even the wind and the water, and they obey Him" (Luke 8:25).

Prepare Your Heart to Hear
Before each of the following six devotional times, quiet your heart and ask God to speak to you personally from His Word. He has the POWER to do it!

Memory Work
Complete your memorization of Luke 9:23-25.

Then He said to them all: "If anyone would come after Me, he must deny himself and take up his cross daily and follow Me. For whoever wants to save his life will lose it, but whoever loses his life for Me will save it. What good is it for a man to gain the whole world, and yet lose or forfeit his very self?"

(When you share your memory work do it in pairs. Also, share if you prayed about showing compassion to someone and if you acted on it. Be honest! If you didn't do either your memory work or your accountability assignment, forgive yourself—but do your memory work at THE THIRD OASIS.)

Warm-Up
Recall some of the times you have PERSONALLY been impacted by the POWER of Jesus: in stopping a storm in your life, in delivering you from fear, or in providing for you. Share one briefly and how it affected your faith in Christ.

Day 1: Overview
1.   Read the Introduction for THE FIFTH STOP! WHO IS THIS WHO STOPS STORMS? (p. 59) and write a summary sentence.

2.   Luke wants us to understand God's power. What does it accomplish in each of the following verses?
    A. Luke 1:35

    B. Luke 4:36

C. Luke 5:17

D. Luke 12:5

E. Luke 21:27

3. Read Luke 8:22 through 9:36 and note instances demonstrating the power of Christ.

Spend five minutes on the memory passage.

Briefly journal what God impressed on your heart today.

Day 2: He Can Calm the Storms in Your Life

Our daughter Sally tells of the storm that came into her life and, consequently, ours, when we adopted Annie, an absolutely adorable five-year-old from an orphanage in Korea:

Until then I'd been the only girl and my parents and brothers lavished attention on me. Suddenly the spotlight turned from me to her, and I felt unloved. I also felt huge and awkward next to this petite little doll. Though

I'd been excited about having a sister, I didn't like her. I didn't want to play with her, talk to her, or be in the same room with her. Everything she did bugged me—even her breathing.

Our sunny Sally soon was exhibiting the signs of a full-blown depression. She wasn't sleeping at night, she was losing weight, and she was overwhelmed by sadness. And Annie was hurt by Sally's rejection. One morning during my quiet time I cried out to the Lord, much like the disciples cried out to Jesus during their storm: "O Lord—I thought You led us to adopt Annie—but I feel like our ship is going down!" Engulfed in self-pity, tears ran down my cheeks. "Lord, help us!"

My husband, who is strong in the Lord and is also a physician acquainted with depression, said: "I think Sally may be suffering from depression and I want to have her tested for a chemical imbalance. But I also realize there is a spiritual problem here, so we need to pray that she will recognize that."

Tests did reveal a chemical imbalance in Sally and after she had been on medication for a month we saw a real change in her. She was sleeping, eating, and even smiling. Sally says:

I felt good enough to go out again. I went to a Christian concert that stirred me deeply. At the closing I went up and knelt at the altar, praying: "Lord, I know I am supposed to love my new sister, but I don't. You know the yuk and jealousy that have been in my heart. O Lord, I am so sorry—but I need Your help. I can't seem to do this on my own. Please take away the yuk and fill me with love for Annie."

Amazingly, God did exactly that. He bent down and listened to that eleven-year-old's cry and filled her with love for her sister. He stopped the storm in our family. The sun came out for Sally, for us, and for little Annie, who, like a drooping flower, began to brighten.

Read Luke 8:22-25.

4. Describe the miracle and the disciples' reaction.

Put yourself in the boat. Describe your thoughts and feelings.

Why do you think they feared Jesus after the storm was calmed?

5. Jesus rebukes the disciples in their fear, saying, in effect, "You should be more trusting." In the midst of pressure, what are some things we should remember about God which will help us to trust?

Is there an application to your life right now? If so, what?

6. A popular Christian song has the lyrics: "Sometimes He calms the storm— and sometimes He calms His child." Share a time when the storm was not stopped—yet God gave you His peace.

Read Psalm 107:23-32.

7. According to the above psalm, who is it who delivers from peril at sea? What else do you see in the psalm?

Meditate on the artist's portrayal of Jesus stopping the storm on page 45. What do you see?

Spend time reviewing your memory passage and write a few sentences in your journal.

Day 3: Be Honest with God—for He Is a God of Power

For twelve years she had suffered the embarrassment of bleeding, a woman's ailment when something is amiss with the menstrual cycle. She was unclean. Shunned. She had spent all she had at the hands of physicians—and only grew worse. (Mark tells us this detail. Luke, the physician, omits it!) Ken Gire, in *Intimate Moments with the Savior,* gives us this portrait:

> *She is destitute now. And being out of money, the doctors finally admit there is nothing they can do for her. Her life is ebbing away. The steady loss of blood over the years has taken its toll. She is anemic, pale, and tired. So very, very tired. . . .*
>
> *She no longer dreams of marriage and a family . . . of combing the hair of a daughter . . . of bouncing a grandbaby on her knee. . . . Her suffering has whisked those dreams into little broken piles.*
>
> *But stories of another physician reach down to pick up the pieces of those dreams. A physician who charges no fee. . . . Who comes not to the strong but to the downtrodden. . . . "if I can find this Jesus and but touch the fringe of his garment. . . . "*[13]

8.   Her emotions must have been strong. Put yourself in her shoes and imagine how you would feel and why at each of these times:
   A. Mark 5:25-26

   B. Mark 5:27-28

   C. Mark 5:29

D. Luke 8:45

E. Luke 8:46

F. Luke 8:47

G. Luke 8:48

This is the only time in the New Testament Jesus calls someone daughter. He is pleased with her faith. She is an example also of courageously testifying to the world of the power of God. May we be like her!

9. Why is it hard to truthfully testify to others about what God has done in our lives?

Why is it hard to be honest with ourselves and with God about the sin in our lives?

Read Psalm 139.

10. Why, according to this psalm, should we be honest with God?

Sometimes we deceive ourselves about our sin. (Jeremiah 17:9 tells us we have deceitful hearts.) What, according to the closing of Psalm 139, should we do about this?

Personal Action Assignment

Pray through Psalm 139:23-24. Be still before the Lord and see what He impresses on your heart. Agree with Him about any sin He reveals. Confess and turn from it.

Day 4: He Has the Power to Provide for Your Every Need

When my husband and I were young, poor, and new in the faith, a missionary asked us to pray about helping to provide her way to Africa. We prayed about it and decided to give her fifty dollars—which seemed like a lot to us. However, when my husband wrote the check, instead of fifty dollars, he wrote out more than twelve times that amount, erroneously writing out the balance in our checkbook! And then he mailed it, oblivious to his error.

Weeks later we received a letter from Africa in which the missionary told us she had wept when she received our check with the exact amount, to the penny, of what she needed. God had moved Steve's hand, though she thought He had moved his heart!

It was only when we read her letter that Steve realized his mistake. Amazingly, none of the checks we had written since then had bounced. And though our balance was tiny, God provided for us over the next few months. A small inheritance check. A gift from friends. Groceries that somehow seemed to stretch.

Is God still in the business of multiplying? Yes, He is! He has the creativity and the *power* to provide when we trust Him.

Read Luke 9:1-17.

11. The basic lesson of this miracle is also taught by Jesus in Matthew 6:31-33. What is it and how can you apply this, right now, to your life?

12. There is also an important lesson for ministry. What did the disciples learn and how could you apply this to ministries to which God has called you?

The most fruitful women's ministries I have known are those which begin by seeking God's idea rather than coming up with their own idea and then asking God to bless it. When we step into what God is already doing, it is like stepping into a raging river, and we experience POWER!

13. If you have had the experience of stepping into God's power in ministry, share something about it.

Jesus models effective teaching in this miracle—and it is not surpising that the disciples never forgot it and it was recorded in all four Gospels. Child Evangelism encourages teachers to act out Bible stories and their lessons with children for they have found: "Children forget what they hear, they remember what they see, and they understand what they do."

14. As a mother, or teacher of children, how could you follow the teaching example of Jesus in Luke 9:10-17?

Choose *one* of the following miracles and brainstorm ways you could teach it so that children would understand the main principle *and* how to apply it to their lives:

        The feeding of the multitudes
        The stopping of the storm

Day 5: But Who Do You Say That I Am?

We have reached the climax and a turning point in Luke. The question is finally articulated. Jesus asks first: "Who do the crowds say I am?" The speculation is that Jesus is from God, yet the crowds have no idea that Jesus is God Incarnate. But do the disciples understand? Jesus turns to Peter, asking him to speak for the men. "But what about you? Who do you say I am?" Peter's reply to this crucial question brings to our mind the regal opening of Luke: the angels, Simeon, Anna—all announcing that this is the Messiah, the Savior, *Christ the Lord.*

Read Luke 9:18-26.

15. What are the people saying? Who do they think Jesus is?

16. There was a popular belief that a prophet of the past would reappear just before the Messiah came. What similarities might they have noticed between Elijah and Jesus? (See 1 Kings 17:10-24) Why would John the Baptist be on their minds? (Luke 9:9)

17. How does Peter answer the question of Jesus?

Though the disciples seem to be realizing that Jesus is the Messiah, they had not yet grasped the concept of a suffering Messiah, and when He suffers, they fall away. How is this seen in:
    A. Luke 18:31-34

    B. Luke 24:13-26

C. Matthew 16:21-23

D. Matthew 26:69-75

Read Luke 9:27-36.

18. How does the incident described in verses 28-36 confirm to the disciples that Peter (not the people) was right about Jesus?

Day 6: Whoever Wants to Save His Life Must Lose It

When my sister lifted up the claims of Christ to me, she said: "Jesus wants you to give Him your whole life."

I responded, "Does this mean that I will have to give up the expensive house Steve and I are planning to build?"

Courageously, my sister said: "It seems to me that you think that house will fill up the emptiness in your life—and only God can do that. Therefore, I think this house is like a god to you and will have to go."

I hesitated. My sister said: "But it will be worth it, Dee. Jesus said that if you try to hold onto your life, you will lose it—but If you give it up for Him, you will find it again. And what does it profit you if you gain the world, including that beautiful house, and lose your soul?"

My sister was absolutely right. And I have often said similar words to a person who is wavering between the broad and the narrow road. One woman asked me: "If I gave my life to Jesus, would I have to stop living with my boyfriend?" I answered much as my sister answered me.

This truth is true not only in salvation, but on a daily basis in living for Christ. No cross—no crown. No discipline—no harvest of righteousness. Whether the discipline involves saying no to the flesh, no to an abortion, no to a dishonest monetary gain, or no to the fears that keep us from being a witness for Christ— so often the wrong choice seems easy at first, but leads to regret—and the right choice seems hard at first but leads to joy and peace.

Share the memory passage and your reflections on it.

19. Can you think of examples of how avoiding suffering or discipline actually leads to greater pain? Or how facing it leads to joy and peace?

20. Be still before the Lord and ask Him to show you how to apply the truth articulated in this verse in your life right now.

21. Jesus gave a near prophecy in verse 27. What was it and how do you see it fulfilled in verses 28-36?

Read Luke 9:37-10:37.

22. What particularly stood out to you from the above section?

Prayer Time

In conversational prayer, lift up your own answer to question 20 audibly and allow two or three other women to say sentence prayers asking God for His help to obey in this area. When there is a pause, another woman should lift up her answer to question 20.

Close with a familiar chorus like "He Is Lord."

the Third Oasis

THE SAVIOR'S WISDOM

He who has ears to hear,
let him hear.
—Luke 14:35

the Third Oasis

The Savior's Wisdom

Luke 10–11; 15

*W*ith Luke 10, the Gospel shifts to "the Jerusalem journey." Jesus begins to teach His disciples intensely, knowing the end is near, and those disciples include women. We will begin this oasis with a careful look at Mary and Martha of Bethany.

Luke *alone* records the incident that occurs in the home of Mary and Martha. Martha is upset that Mary is not helping her in the kitchen. But instead of rebuking Mary, instead of brushing her into the kitchen, Jesus firmly protects her choice, saying, "Mary has chosen what is better, and it will not be taken away from her" (Luke 10:42).

Only men were to sit at the feet of a rabbi (the women were to learn at home from their men)! Jesus is revolutionary in the way He treats women, turning upside down the accepted attitude toward women. His attitude was different from the disciples, different from His contemporaries, different, even, from the attitude of many Christians today toward women. Dorothy Sayers put it like this: "A teacher who never nagged at them, who never flattered or coaxed or patronized; who never made arch jokes about them . . . who took their questions and arguments seriously."[14]

Jesus certainly took Mary of Bethany seriously, and she Him. She alone among the disciples understood that He was going to die. Should we not learn from this unusual woman?

For the next four weeks, as you journey through His wisdom, diligently prac-tice Mary's habit of sitting at His feet on a daily basis. Choose the same place and the same time each day—strive to listen, not just to complete your daily assignment. This WISDOM OASIS is filled with practical teachings on priorities, prayer, and parables! God has something of immense value for you personally, each day. Don't miss it! Jesus tells us: "He who has ears to hear, let him hear" (Luke 14:35).

Sixth Stop!
Mary of Bethany

John (John 11:5) mentions that Jesus loved these three siblings: Mary, Martha, and Lazarus. The evidence is strong that they were some of His closest friends and that He visited them often, particularly now, as He is honing in on Jerusalem, for Bethany was an easy walk (1 and 3/4 miles) from the Holy City. I like to think that the One who had no home and "no place to lay His head" (Luke 9:58) found some comfort here. In order to see the whole picture we will begin in Luke, but then travel to the Gospel of John.

I have known a few women like Mary of Bethany. My older sister Sally always begins her day in hours of prayer and study and then asks: "Lord, this is Your day. Your plans are best. How would You have me spend it?" Because of her listening heart, God has given her incredible wisdom and timing. She knew exactly the right time, more than thirty years ago, to visit me and lift up the claims of Christ. God used Sally's visit to bring me and my husband to Christ.

Ten years later my husband and I asked God, unless He had a better idea, to give us a daughter who had a spiritually tender heart like that of her Aunt Sally, like that of Mary of Bethany! God graciously answered our prayers, and we named her Sally. Even as a little girl our daughter thirsted for God. As she grew older I would often ask, like Martha, for Sally's help in the kitchen. So often Sally would say: "I'd be glad to, Mom—but first may I have my time with the Lord?" And that time would often stretch into an hour or two. Last month, a few hours before her morning wedding, I found this undistracted bride spending the early hours with Jesus.

Women like Mary of Bethany are rare. Not only are they wiser than most of us, they radiate a peace and a joy that comes from being with Jesus.

Prepare Your Heart to Hear

Each day, choose to sit at Jesus' feet, asking Him to help you hear "your portion" for the day.

Memory Work

In this wisdom oasis you will learn Luke 10:38-42. This week learn Luke 10:38-39:

> **As Jesus and His disciples were on their way, He came to a village where a woman named Martha opened her home to Him. She had a sister called Mary, who sat at the Lord's feet listening to what He said.**

Warm-Up

Overcoming distractions is a common problem for women who tend to have many roles. What kind of things typically distract you, keeping you from sitting at the Lord's feet and listening?

Day 1: Overview

1.   Read all of the introductory notes. Comment on what stood out to you from:

A. The Introductory notes for THE THIRD OASIS: THE SAVIOR'S WISDOM (p. 72)

B. The Introductory notes for THE SIXTH STOP! MARY OF BETHANY (p. 73)

Spend five minutes on the memory passage.

In your personal quiet time sing: "As the Deer" or "Breathe on Me, Breath of God" from your hymnal.

Day 2: Overview Continued

2.   Read the following passages about Mary and Martha. Write down any initial observations that you have about each:

   A. Luke 10:38-42

   Mary   *Martha*

   B. John 11:1 through John 12:11

   Mary   *Martha*

Review the memory passage.

Day 3: In Quietness and Confidence Shall Be Your Strength

Amy Shreve-Wixtrom reminds me of Mary of Bethany. Even though she performs before thousands, Amy is actually an introvert, drawing strength from time alone, sitting at the feet of Jesus. Read carefully Amy's lyrics to "Martha's Song":

Martha's Song
Amy Shreve-Wixtrom

With a million things expecting His attention
Jesus took the time to meet us in our home
There were so many people here to ask Him questions
And my sister, Mary, left me all the work to do alone

Well, I've always been responsible and helpful
Mary just gets lost in what she wants to see
But when I complained of her unwillingness to help me
Jesus said she chose the better part,
simply sitting at His feet

Just to be closer to Jesus
Just to be near His sweet voice
To bask in His presence my cares all fade into joy
Just to be closer to Jesus
Receiving the peace He imparts
I want to want most of all
Just to be near His heart.

With a million things demanding my attention
I realize now that Mary knew a precious thing
There's no accomplishment or praise that can compare to
Leaving all my worries far behind & simply worshiping my King.

3.   What "precious thing" did Mary of Bethany know? Explain why Mary's priorities were better.

Review your memory verse. The word that J.B. Phillips paraphrases "bothered" in Luke 10:41 is also translated "upset or troubled." It comes from the Greek word turbazo *(emotionally stirred up). Our words "tumultuous" and "turbulent" come from this Greek word.*

4.   What images or word pictures do the words "tumultuous" or "turbulent" bring to your mind?

5.   What do you learn from the following Scriptures?
      A. Psalm 46:10

      B. Ecclesiastes 4:6

      C. Isaiah 30:15

      D. Psalm 131:1-2

Dr. S. Conway[15] has given me insight into the imagery of "a child weaned from its mother." A loving mother gently weans her child from the breast to the cup. Though he loved the breast, in time, the very desire for the breast is gone—he is happy and content. Likewise, God longs to wean us from the world, to help us to be content with what He has for us.

6.   How does the word picture from Psalm 131 of "stilling and quieting your soul like a weaned child with its mother" speak to you?

      From what might you need to be weaned in order to have time for the Lord?

      How do you go about quieting yourself when you meet with God?

From what might you need to be weaned to live wholeheartedly for Christ?

Read 1 Timothy 2:1-4.

7.   How could a mother help her children to lead "quiet lives"?

Family nights, the limiting of extracurricular activity, and homeschooling are all ways Christian families are endeavoring to return to the quiet life. It is also key that we help our children discover the joy of reading, crafts, and the outdoors. My research has shown me that the families who are most successful with this have severely limited television watching. Here is one testimony:

> *Both my parents grew up in homes where the television was the center of family life. It was on during dinner, it provided the background noise throughout the day. When my folks got married, they decided they wanted to raise their children in a TV-free home. . . . In my parents' opinion, the primary problem with TV isn't the bad things that are watched, it's the good things you're not doing because you're watching—the books that go unread and the stories that go untold. I'm thankful my parents chose books and conversations over television.[16]*

8. Have you tamed the beast of television so it won't rob you of what is best? If so, how?

Day 4: A Trusting Heart

As I am growing in the Lord I am realizing more and more how mysterious He is. So often He doesn't make sense to me until much later—and sometimes, not even then. I tend to be like Martha, arguing with His plan. ("'But, Lord,' said

Martha, the sister of the dead man, 'by this time there is a bad odor, for he has been there four days,'" John 11:39.)

Not Mary of Bethany. She doesn't argue, but trusts. And she is given more light than any of the disciples. O Lord, help me to trust You like Mary of Bethany!

Read John 11:1-44 carefully.

9. Read John 11:1-3 again:
    A. How does John open the story of the raising of Lazarus with the spotlight on the sisters, especially Mary?

    B. The sisters faced a dilemma. If they asked Jesus to come, they were putting His life in danger (see John 11:8); yet if they didn't, they were putting the life of their beloved brother in danger. How do they handle it?

    C. How might this be a model when we are uncertain as to how to pray?

10. Even though their brother's death is not what they wanted, find evidence that each sister trusted Christ.

11. Sometimes God does not make sense. What do you learn from Romans 11:33-34 concerning the ways of the Lord?

Personal Action Assignment

In your journal, tell Jesus about areas of concern in your life as Mary and Martha did (John 11:1-3). Don't tell Him *what* to do, but ask for His help.

Day 5: God Reveals Mysteries to Those Who Hunger and Thirst

Scripture makes it clear that those who hunger and thirst for God are given *more* light. Mary of Bethany understood what all of the other disciples missed.

12. Read Luke 18:31-34 and describe the disciples' understanding of the prophecy which Jesus gave.

13. Read John 12:1-11.
    A. In verses 3 through 6, contrast the illumined heart of Mary with the darkened heart of Judas.

    B. Jesus defends Mary, as He did in Luke 10:42. What does He say about her in John 12:7-8?

14. At what point do you imagine Mary understood Jesus was going to die? (Choose one of these times or another and explain your thinking: Luke 10:39; John 11:44, 53; 12:1-2.)

Mary understood that Jesus was going to the cross. Today that event has already happened, yet many still, though they know Jesus died on a cross, do not understand *why* He did or what it has to do with them *personally*. In one sentence explain when and how you came to understand this truth.

Day 6: She Did What She Could

Mary not only listened, she responded to the wisdom God gave her. She understood Jesus was headed to Jerusalem to die and so she took a precious flask of perfume and boldly broke it to anoint Jesus for His burial. Having been given wisdom, she acted on it. She seized the moment and did what she could.

Read John 12:18 again.

15. In all three pictures that we have of Mary of Bethany (Luke 10, John 11, and John 12) she is in the same physical position. What is it?

16. Many confuse this incident when Mary of Bethany anointed Jesus for His burial with the incident recorded in Luke 7:36-50. What evidence can you give for these being two separate incidents with very different lessons?

Both of these incidents occurred in the home of "Simon." However, in Luke, early in Jesus' ministry, a woman with a sinful past comes to the home of Simon the Pharisee. (Luke's emphasis is that salvation is available to all.) Here, in John, the incident is a different one. Mary of Bethany comes to the home of Simon the Leper, late in Jesus' ministry, to anoint Jesus for His burial. (John's emphasis is that Jesus is the Christ.)

17. Describe what each sister is doing in this account. Do you think one act was more encouraging than the other? If so, why?

Speaker Diane Strack tells of visiting an art museum and seeing a painting of Jesus on the cross. Below that painting was another painting of Mary of Bethany anointing Christ with perfume. Mrs. Strack commented that Mary's act helped Jesus to find the strength to go to the cross. Therefore, though Martha's meeting of Jesus' physical needs was important, she believes that here again Mary chose the best.

18. Mary of Bethany acted on the insight God gave her. What do you learn from the following about seizing the moment?
    A. Proverbs 3:27-28

    B. Ecclesiastes 11:4-6

19. Brainstorm times when you could be bolder, seize the moment, and make a difference.

    One obvious parallel is letting your loved ones know how much you care before they die. Have you done this? Be still before the Lord and ask Him if there is something you should do. If He impresses something on you, do it now! Then write down what you did to encourage others in the study group.

20. What have you learned from the model of Mary of Bethany? (Be specific.) How could you apply this to your life?

Prayer Time
Lift up your answer to question 20 in prayer and let the other women support you with sentence prayers. When there is a silence, another woman should lift up her request.

Close with a familiar chorus such as "O How He Loves You and Me."

Seventh Stop!
Martha of Bethany

She had the gifts of a Martha Stewart, the woman whose name has become synonymous with the ultimate in homemaking. I can picture Martha of Bethany stenciling daisies on the disciples' lunch bags, placing a glowing bayberry candle in the room where Jesus slept, and serving Him fresh fish crepes garnished with rosecut strawberries for breakfast. Certainly Martha of Bethany had a gift for serving, but that gift had a tendency to engulf her, causing her to miss what was most important.

It happens to us all the time. We take care of the physical needs of our families, but miss the bread that will last. We get our hair, makeup, and dress ready for church and enter worship uptight and distracted because we have forgotten to prepare our hearts. We bring our families *CHRISTMAS,* but the Christ Child is lost beneath the wrappings.

It is wonderful to grace our lives with love and aesthetic beauty, and when we do it as a gift to others, it can soothe and warm the heart. As women, we have that natural gift—yet we need to learn what is most important.

For many years my sympathies lay with Martha because I empathized with how difficult it would be to get lunch ready for thirteen hungry men all by myself. But if you look at the pronouns carefully, you will see that though the disciples came near to Bethany, they probably stayed elsewhere than at this family's home. Martha "opened her home to Him." In *The Book of God, The Bible as a Novel,* Walter Wangerin imagines it from the perspective of Mary of Bethany:

During these last three years He has usually come in the company of His disciples. He first makes sure that they all have food and places to sleep in Bethany, then He slips silently into our courtyard.

. . . Martha bustled into the house, her arms full, her cheeks jiggling with haste and work and pleasure.

"I told Lazarus that the Master was here," she announced. "He'll be coming over for cakes," she said. "So much, so much to do!"

. . . Soon the fresh oil was crackling and we began to smell fish. Where had she found fish so early in the morning?

"My sister," I called out loud. "The miracle worker!"

There came a sudden thump, dough thrown on a wooden board. When I turned, I saw Martha standing behind me, her fists on her hips, her expression hard and dark.[17]

Martha reminds me of Peter. She is strong, outspoken, and bold. Both Peter and Martha had moments when they disagreed with Jesus and let Him know it! Yet, Peter and Martha also had teachable hearts. When they were rebuked by Jesus, they repented. Jesus blessed them for their teachable hearts by revealing *more* light to them. Peter and Martha are the followers who make a bold confession of faith, coming to the realization that Jesus is "the Christ of God." (Peter's confession is in Luke 9:20 and Martha's is in John 11:27.)

When we first meet Martha, she is angry that her younger sister is not helping her. She presumes not only to correct Mary, but to imply that Jesus does not care enough about her or He would have chastised Mary.

Jesus surprises Martha by chastising her. I can see a gentle smile playing around His lips as He says:

Martha, Martha . . . you are worried and upset about many things, but only one thing is needed (Luke 10:41-42).

Martha was apparently preparing many courses, many dishes. Charles Swindoll paraphrases, "Martha, Martha—we came for the fellowship, not for the food. Chips and dips would be fine!"[18] Secondly, there is a wordplay on the phrase "one dish" or "portion." Jesus often contrasts the bread of this world with the bread of life. Our portion, the psalmist tells us, is "the Word of God." Mary had chosen that portion, and Jesus protects her from her sister by saying:

Mary has chosen what is better, and it will not be taken away from her (Luke 10:42).

Martha is working on a five-course meal, but Mary has chosen the "main course" and *that* is what is most important. In this situation, simplicity in hospitality was called for, for Jesus had dropped in, not to eat a big meal, but to teach them.

Prepare Your Heart to Hear
Each day, choose to sit at Jesus' feet, asking Him to help you hear "your portion" for the day.

Memory Work
Add verse 40 to Luke 10:38-39.

> **As Jesus and His disciples were on their way, He came to a village where a woman named Martha opened her home to Him. She had a sister called Mary, who sat at the Lord's feet listening to what He said. But Martha was distracted by all the preparations that had to be made. She came to Him and asked, "Lord, don't You care that my sister has left me to do the work by myself? Tell her to help me!"**

Warm-Up
Finish this sentence:

When I am a guest, what ministers to me most is when the hostess

_____ .

Day 1: Overview
1. Read Luke 10:38-42 slowly. Read the introductory notes for THE SEVENTH STOP! MARTHA OF BETHANY (pp. 83-85). What stood out to you? Why?

2.   Read John 11:1 through 12:11 carefully. Do you see anything you haven't seen before? If so, share what it is and why it impresses you.

Review your memory passage.

Day 2: Don't You Care?

Sometimes God's ways are so different from our ways. And sometimes, because He seems silent or slow or mysterious—we find ourselves wondering if He cares. I have often clung to the wisdom of the late Paul Little who spoke at Moody's Founder's Week shortly before he was killed in an automobile accident. Prophetically, Little said:

> I do a lot of traveling—and I may die before what people consider to be my time. But if that happens, don't ask, "Why?" Ask, "Is God good?" And we know God is good, for He died for us.

That is the truth to which we must cling when it appears God has forgotten us. Martha had not seen Jesus raise her brother from the dead—nor had she seen Him die for her. After that, I suspect that she knew, even when God seemed silent, or slow, or mysterious—that He cared for her.

3.   In the following instances, how does Martha question the actions of Jesus and imply that they show a lack of caring?
    A. Luke 10:40

    B. John 11:21

    C. John 11:39

4.   What evidence do you see of a change in Martha in John 12?

Peter, the disciple who is so like Martha, learned that though the ways of God may be strange, they are best. And an older and wiser Peter exhorts us: "Cast all your anxiety on Him because He cares for you" (1 Peter 5:7).

Personal Action Assignment

Is there a situation in your life right now in which you need to remember that Jesus cares for you? Cast your anxiety on Him. Record this in your journal.

Day 3: Overcoming the Distractions

One woman said: "When I sit down with the Lord, Satan whispers: 'Just put a load of wash in.' So, I hop up and put a load of wash in. Then I sit down and he will whisper: 'Just clear the dishes.' Then the phone rings and somehow, I never get back to the Lord. Now I recognize the enemy's voice and shut him out. God is first in my life, so I get up before the children and spend time with Him. He comes before housework, before reading the paper, before anything!"

5.   If you have learned some methods which help you overcome distractions in your prayer or Bible study time, please share.

Review your memory passage.

6.   The same root word which is used in Luke 10:40 concerning Martha "who was *distracted* by all the preparations" is used in 1 Corinthians 7:34-35 as "undistracted" or "undivided." Read 1 Corinthians 7:32-35. According to this passage, what can be an advantage of being single?

7. If we fail to listen to the Lord, we may actually be working at cross-purposes with Him, though it seems like we are serving Him. How was this true of Martha in the Luke passage?

Personal Action Assignment

In your journal, write down your two most important life goals, based on Luke 10:27. Be still before the Lord. Are your daily priorities in line with these goals, or have you become distracted by transitory things? Write down any changes you sense God impresses you to make.

Sing "Seek Ye First."

Now, prayerfully make your "to do" list for the day (or, if you have your quiet time in the evening, for tomorrow). After listing what you hope to accomplish, highlight what is most important to God and make sure you do those things.

Day 4: Don't Forget the Main Course

My friend Carol Gangwish often will invite women over for a lovely three course luncheon when their children head back to school in the fall, or to celebrate Christ's birth or resurrection. During those luncheons, Carol never forgets "the main course." We share how God is working in our lives and we pray. And Carol is also sensitive enough to the Spirit to know that there are times when she needs to welcome someone into her home on the spot, open a can of Campbell's soup (though Carol probably has homemade soup in her freezer!), and concentrate on the Bread of Life.

Read Luke 10:38-42 carefully. Review your memory passage.

8. Looking carefully at Luke 10, answer the following:
    Verse 41a: How does the repetition indicate tenderness? (Compare Luke 13:34 and 22:31.)

Verse 42: What does Jesus say about Mary? (How is this similar to Psalm 119:57?)

9. In Luke 4:4, Jesus quotes Deuteronomy 8:3. What does that say and how does it relate to this incident?

10. Brainstorm ways you could "remember the main course" when you are doing the following things:
    A. Having dinner with your family

    B. Braiding your daughter's hair

    C. Walking with a friend

Day 5: There Is a Time to Be Simple and a Time to Be Elaborate

As I study hospitality in Scripture, the overall emphasis *seems to be on simplicity so that we can practice hospitality regularly.* We are all to be welcoming the newcomer, the missionary, the spiritually or emotionally needy friend into our homes! There is a time for elaborate preparations, but generally, we are to keep it simple. If we take on what God does not ask us to take on (such as fixing an elaborate meal for a drop-in guest), we may find ourselves grumbling!

11. How might the following verses have given Martha perspective that day? And, what do they say to you?
    A. 1 Peter 4:9

B. Proverbs 15:17

C. Proverbs 17:1

12. There is, however, an appropriate time for elaborate preparations. In Scripture, this was often done in connection with a special occasion *in order* to celebrate or remember God's goodness! How do you see this in the following?
    A. When revival came, what were the people instructed to do in Nehemiah 8:10-12?

    B. When the Jews were delivered from a holocaust, what did they do in Esther 9:18-19?

    C. Sometimes holiday preparations are elaborate, but "the main course" (God) is forgotten. What does the Lord say about this in Isaiah 1:14-17?

13. Sometimes "Martha-like" preparations are appropriate to encourage the heart or to enhance the meaning of a holiday. For example, along with candy eggs, you might hide plastic Easter eggs with symbols of a sponge, a cross, a rooster, etc. and then ask children to explain them. Give an example of a "Martha-like" preparation to enhance a baby shower, a neighborhood Christmas coffee, or family devotions.

Day 6: A Teachable Heart

Often women who discuss Luke 11:38-41 defend Martha, even though Jesus chastised her. This is inappropriate and leans toward an unteachable heart. However, we should not color Martha's whole life by one incident, for that *is* unfair. Elwood McQuaid points out that though Martha did have a case of temporarily misplaced priorities, she loved the Lord deeply.[19] There aren't many functional families in the Bible—but the Bethany family shines! Martha shows her godliness in her servant spirit, in her hospitality, and in her confession of faith.

Read John 11.

14. In John 11,
    A. How do you see Martha struggling to trust in verses 21-24?

    B. How does Jesus strengthen Martha's faith and how does she respond positively in verses 25-28?

    C. Jesus brings light to our darkness when He sees a pure and seeking heart. How do you see this in verses 32-44?

15. In John 12, when her sister pours expensive perfume on Jesus, the disciples object, but Martha is silent. How do you think she felt?

16. What do you learn about the relationship between the heart attitude and the ability to receive wisdom from the following?
    A. Psalm 25:14-15

B. Psalm 101:2

C. Luke 11:9-10

D. Romans 1:21-28

E. James 1:5-6

17. What has God impressed on your heart from the example of Martha of Bethany and what application will you make?

Prayer Time

Instead of sharing individual prayer requests, have each woman lift her own request up in prayer. Then have a few women support her with sentences. When there is a silence, another woman should lift up her individual prayer request.

Eighth Stop!
Praying Effectively

Our sons were out of the nest and it wouldn't be long before our daughters took flight as well. I thought my husband and I were entering a new phase of life when he surprised me:

Steve: I think we should adopt again. (We had adopted our youngest daughter, Annie, from Korea.)

I laughed.

Steve: We're finally getting good at parenting—why should we stop now?

I was speechless.

Steve: The overseas orphanages are teeming with children. Let's call Holt International Children's Services and tell them that we're ready for a challenge: an older child, a handicapped child, or a sibling group.

Me: I don't think so.

Steve: Would you be willing to pray about it?

Me: (With great hesitancy.) OK.

Steve: Great! Let's go into the living room right now and kneel before God. Let's try to get rid of our own desires and seek His desire.

And so began my refining journey into the heart of God. I will tell you about our journey in this lesson as we examine the Savior's wisdom, as relayed by Luke, on praying effectively.

Prepare Your Heart to Hear
Each day, choose to sit at Jesus' feet, asking Him to help you hear "your portion" for the day. For those reading through all of Luke, do the extra credit each day.

Memory Work
Complete your memory work of Luke 10:38-42. (If you have fallen behind, memorize the second paragraph only.)

> **As Jesus and His disciples were on their way, He came to a village where a woman named Martha opened her home to Him. She had a sister called Mary, who sat at the Lord's feet listening to what He said. But Martha was distracted by all the preparations that had to be made. She came to Him and asked, "Lord, don't You care that my sister has left me to do the work by myself? Tell her to help me!"**
>
> **"Martha, Martha," the Lord answered, "you are worried and upset about many things, but only one thing is needed. Mary has chosen what is better, and it will not be taken away from her."**

Warm-Up
What is one of the nicest gifts you have ever given to someone? Why did you do it?

Day 1: Approaching God in Humility

Elisa Morgan, President of M.O.P.S. International (Mothers-of-Preschoolers), gives a wonderful dramatization of our arrogance in approaching God as if He is a vending machine. "We put in our three minutes of prayer, we wait three minutes, and then we say 'Where are the goods?'" (Wildly, she starts kicking the machine.)

When my husband challenged me to seek God's will concerning a child, I was fearful. What if God's desire was different from mine? I had given my life to the Lord. Yet now I had to consider the state of my heart.

Was I the Lord's servant? Or had I begun arrogantly treating the Lord as if He were my servant?

Read Luke 18:9-14

1. Contrast:	*The Pharisee*	*The Tax Collector*
Attitude		
Motive		
Subject (God or self)		
Effectiveness before God		

An anonymous Russian book of the nineteenth century, The Way of a Pilgrim, *tells how Christians formed the habit of saying the "Jesus Prayer": "Lord Jesus*

Christ, have mercy on me." Inspired by this parable, they tried to learn to say this prayer constantly in the back of their minds, no matter what they were doing. To remind themselves some wore a piece of knotted yarn around a wrist. . . . [20]

Personal Action Assignment

Look up *mercy* in a dictionary. Then tie a string around your wrist to remind you to pray, throughout the day, "Lord Jesus Christ, have mercy on me." Tomorrow, record in this space how saying this impacted your attitude and why.

Extra Credit

Read Luke 11:14-54. One of the most effective ways to pray is to pray through Scripture. Here, for example, you might be inspired to pray for protection from demons (verses 14-26), for obedience (verses 27-28), light (verses 33-36), love, and justice (verses 37-54) in your life.

Begin learning the memory passage.

Day 2: Approaching God in Trust

When my husband and I knelt before the Lord, I didn't hear anything. No Scripture verses came to mind. No strong impression came to my heart. Silence.

After what seemed like a long time I looked up. My husband had a stunned look. I said, "What is it?"

He said: "Maybe I imagined it."

"What?"

"While we were praying, I saw a young girl crying."

I was quiet. My husband was not given to hearing voices or seeing visions.

Steve stood and said, "Let's just wait a few days and see how God works."

A few days later, the phone rang. When I heard Barbara Kim's voice I began to feel like the canoe I was in had turned the bend and was now rushing toward the rapids. Barbara worked with Holt International Services. She was excited, having just returned from a trip to an orphanage in Bangkok, Thailand. This was our conversation as I remember it:

Barbara: Dee, we have chosen 12 children out of 500 from that orphanage—children who have spirits of survival. There was one little girl who stole our hearts—and several of us thought of your family.

Me: Why?

Barbara: She reminded us of your oldest daughter. Like Sally, Beth is charming and winsome. All that's wrong with her is that she's missing an arm. It was amputated and she was abandoned as a baby. She's almost ten. Could we send you her picture? Would you be willing to pray?

Me: (with hesitancy) OK. Send the picture. We will pray.

When the envelope arrived I propped it up on the dinner table and waited for Steve to come home. I prayed. I paced. Finally Steve came home and opened the envelope with trembling hands. When a picture of a beautiful young girl fell out, Steve stared at her face. "Yes. This is the little girl whose face I saw."

My heart froze. Didn't God know that I had a full plate? Didn't He care about me and my life?

Again, I had to examine my attitude. Was I willing to lay down my agenda for His? Did I trust that God loved me and knew what was best?

Record your response to yesterday's action assignment.

Read Luke 12:22-34.

2. Describe how each of the following passages shows God's care for us. Write the principle taught in each.
   A. Luke 12:24

   B. Luke 12:27-28

C. Luke 12:29-32

D. Jeremiah 29:11-13

3. Think of examples from the last few weeks that show God's care for you. Record them in your journal and share one with the group.

Extra Credit
Read and pray through Luke 12:8-21.

Close your personal quiet time with "God Is So Good."

Day 3: Approaching the Lord with Faith

The picture of a person seeking and knocking on a door is given to describe coming to God in salvation—but then, also, after salvation, coming to God daily to seek His face. He is on the other side of the door. He *exists* and He *rewards* those who earnestly seek Him (Hebrews 11:6).

4. The image of a door (or gate) in salvation helps us to understand a few key concepts. Discover them in these passages:
    A. John 10:19

    B. Luke 13:22-30

In his powerful preaching, Billy Graham often talked about the door of salvation. "It is open now, but one day, it will be shut—and no man will be able to open it."[21]

5.   There is also an image of a door concerning communication with the Lord. He longs for a love relationship with us, just as the new husband longs to be with his bride. What mistake does she make in Song of Songs 5:2-6 when he knocks on the door? Why? Application?

6.   Just as we are to seek the Lord in salvation, we are to seek Him on a daily basis. Rather than treating God like a vending machine, we are to seek His face, His desires—before we ask. Review Luke 12:29-34 and comment:

   A. Contrast the object of the pagan's search with the object of a wise child of God.

   B. Discuss Psalm 37:4. What does this mean? (Luke 12:34 may help you understand how this occurs.)

   C. Has God ever changed the desires of your heart? If so, share how you think it happened.

Extra Credit
Read and pray through Luke 12:35-59.

Close your personal quiet time with "Change My Heart, O God."

Day 4: Lord, Teach Us to Pray

Concerning the "Lord's Prayer," Dr. Darrell Bock says:

> *Perhaps the most ignored feature of the prayer is that it is a community prayer, not an individual one. Provision, forgiveness, and protection are asked for the community. The lesson of the Lord's Prayer is that we pray not just for the individual, but also for the community, for the spiritual benefit of all who know God.*[22]

We are to be praying for our brothers and sisters in Christ, and this prayer shows us how!

In my quest for peace in adopting Beth, the community of believers played a large part. In particular, three sisters in Christ prayed for me and for our whole family. Each woman sought God's face. It is interesting to me to reflect back and to see how their attitudes in approaching the Lord reflected the principles Jesus taught in Luke 11:2-3.

For example, my soul mate Shell refused to give me advice off the top of her head. Instead, she asked for the morning to seek the Lord. She knew that God was holy ("hallowed be Your name") and so she took her responsibility of counseling me very seriously. She also understood the second principle of the Lord's Prayer ("Thy kingdom come . . . "). When we come to God, it should not be to give Him orders, but to ask Him how we can fit in with His plans for making this world more like His kingdom. Shell asked, "How can the Brestins best fit into Your plan, Lord?" The blueprints for bringing the kingdom to earth are in His Word, so Shell prayerfully searched the Scriptures. Finally, Shell wrote me a ten-page letter filled with Scripture. (I never realized how many Scriptures there were concerning caring for the fatherless and submitting to your husband!)

7. In Luke 11:1-4 find and put in your own words:
    A. The address

    B. The two statements

C. The three petitions

8. Against what wrong attitudes does Ecclesiastes 5:1-2 warn? What right attitudes does Luke 11:2 teach?

How did Dee's friend Shell exemplify the right attitude?

My next friend, Sara, also helped me to understand the sinfulness in my own heart and how it was impacting me. Jeremiah tells us we have deceitful hearts. This is one of the reasons we need each other in the community of believers—to help us to see our blind spots! Solomon says the purposes of our hearts are like dark waters —but a friend of understanding can draw those waters out (Proverbs 20:5). After prayer, Sara probed to try to understand why I was reluctant. This was our conversation:

Sara: Are you afraid because of her age? Do you think that because she is almost ten that it's too late to mold her?

Me: No. I can't imagine taking a baby or a toddler. I'm too tired! I'm *glad* she's almost ten.

Sara: Are you afraid that because she is missing an arm that you will forever be helping her?

Me: No. Steve tells me that those who've been without a limb for a long time have learned how to do practically everything for themselves.

Then I began to share with Sara that my husband, who is an orthopedic surgeon, had said Beth would do some things with her feet and her teeth. I began to cry, admitting to Sara that it would embarrass me. At that moment we both realized that at least part of my hesitancy was due to an unmerciful attitude.

Again and again, Luke shows us that Jesus is longing for those who say they belong to God to live lives of purity and mercy. He is angry at the Pharisees for their hypocrisy. He weeps over Jerusalem. He pleads with His listeners to live lives that reflect God's kingdom! As my friends prayed for me, God revealed the impurity and hardness of my heart.

How we need to continually be praying for one another in the body of Christ, not in a rote way, with meaningless memorized phrases, but with passion that God's holiness and mercy will grow in our collective hearts!

O God, You are our FATHER! May we live like Your children!

O God, You are HOLY! May we be holy!

O God, bring Your heavenly KINGDOM to earth. Use us as Your vessels to do so!

And then, Father, please:
PROVIDE for us
PARDON us and empower us to truly pardon others
PROTECT us from the wiles of the evil one.

9. Jesus was angry when those who claimed to belong to God were filled with darkness. He urged believers to live holy lives. Summarize His exhortation in each of the following:
A. Luke 6:27-31

B. Luke 6:46

C. Luke 11:42

D. Luke 12:1-7

Extra Credit
Read and pray through Luke 13:1-21.

Personal Action Assignment

Confess and turn from sin in your life. Then intercede for the body of Christ (perhaps for particular leaders, your home church . . .) in your community, using the Lord's Prayer to guide you. Record your requests in your journal.

Day 5: Approaching the Lord Boldly

When I repented of my selfishness and asked God to change my heart, His grace began to flow. Part of that grace was my friend Janet who told me that if we adopted Beth, she would love to help me. She said that Beth could come to her home daily to learn English. By now I had not only a peace, but an excitement.

That didn't mean that our adoption journey was easy! There were plenty of times when we came boldly to the Lord asking Him to tame a new lion that had sprung out in our path!

One lion was my schedule. I was booked to be the keynote speaker at women's conferences three out of four weekends. We were told that on short notice we would need to fly to Thailand and stay there for two weeks. Anxious thoughts filled my heart. "How could I break my word to these conferences at the last minute? And yet, if I didn't, how would our new daughter (and the Thai adoption officials!) feel if Steve came alone?"

I am hesitant to dictate specific requests to God, for who am I to tell the One who made the universe what to do? And yet, He was my Father and I needed help! Alan Redpath has pointed out that prayer should be more than just asking God to bless some folks and keep us plugging along, prayer is warfare![23]

As I looked through my calendar I found a two-week free period, beginning February 14th. And so, I said: "Lord, unless You have a better idea, could we please be asked to fly to Thailand on February 14th?"

The parable Jesus tells in Luke 11 fits perfectly here. For years I thought the point was persistence. It's not, though a persistent person may have this quality. See if you can discern the main point of the parable.

Read Luke 11:5-8.

10. Think about a time when you were in a tight spot, as the unprepared host was in this parable, or as Dee was in the above story. You had to have help. Recall the situation, your feelings, and why you dared to ask a stranger or a friend for help.

11. Describe the embarrassing situation in Luke 11:6.

In biblical times, it was a disgrace to be a poor host. You couldn't call Pizza Hut to deliver. The difficulty here is magnified by the midnight hour. Not only was his neighbor asleep, he had a wife and small children who were asleep in the bed with him. (Not uncommon in those days.) Perhaps the children were colicky babies who had been rocked and rocked. Finally . . . the whole family is asleep. There is humor in this story. What a spot for the unprepared host! Will he dare to go and bang on his neighbor's door? Amazingly, he does. It is so important to him to be a good host that he does. It took nerve!

12. What does the host decide to do? What word do you think best describes him?

   Why does his neighbor get out of bed?

In the Greek the word translated importunity or boldness is *anaideia* which has a sense of shamelessness.

13. Share a time when you were BOLD in prayer and God answered.

Extra Credit
Read and pray through Luke 13:31–14:24.

Day 6: Approaching the Lord Persistently
On January 20th, we got the phone call from Holt.

Barbara: "Pack your bags, Dee! It's time for you and Steve to go get your daughter!"

I held my breath. "When?"

Barbara: "February 1st!"

My heart dropped. I had been bold, but God seemed to be saying no. I knew I couldn't go to Thailand—I had committed to three retreats in the first two weeks of February. The authorities in Thailand agreed our daughter Sally could go in my place and, with a heavy heart, I bought airplane tickets for my husband and daughter.

Frankly, it didn't even occur to me to *keep on* praying for February 14th— I thought that door was shut! But the women who were coordinating a retreat I was giving in Wichita in early February felt badly that I had to be with them instead of in Thailand. So *they* persisted in prayer and encouraged me to persist. We prayed the authorities in Thailand would change their minds and postpone the date for two weeks!

A few days before Steve and Sally were to leave, Barbara called and asked: "Dee, is there any chance you could go on February 14th? Thailand has postponed your date by two weeks!"

I changed the dates of the tickets (we had not originally planned to take Sally—but she proved crucial in helping Beth feel at ease) and I bought a third ticket for me. I have thanked God so many times for allowing me to go. I will never forget Beth's radiant face when we met her. This was a child who, at the time Steve and I prayed, had given up hope of ever having a home and was despairing. It overwhelms me to realize God heard her cry. A little girl who is not valued in our world, is of great value to God. In part, this is the message of Luke.

Review your memory passage.

Read Luke 18:1-8.

14. In the Parable of the Persistent Widow:
    A. Why does Jesus tell this parable according to verse 1?

    B. Describe the character of the judge in verses 2 and 4.

    C. Describe the character of God in Luke 11:11-13. Contrast the character of God with the judge in this parable.

    D. Describe the character of the widow in Luke 18:3 and 5.

    E. If you are a widow or a single mom, can you understand why she might have been so persistent? If so, share.

    F. What lesson does Jesus give in Luke 18:6-8?

    "Persistent prayer serves the purpose of strengthening our resolve." [24]

15. Summarize the right attitudes for effective prayer as taught in this lesson. What are they? How has God spoken to you?

Extra Credit
Read and pray through Luke 14:25-35.

Prayer Time
On an index card, write down a bold request that seems as if it would be in line with God's will. Place the cards in the middle of the table, pray, and take one.

Ninth Stop!
Parables That Women Love

How we love the Parable of the Prodigal Son! Prodigals all, we bathe in the warmth and comfort of the Father's love:

But when he was yet a great way off, his father saw him, and had compassion, and ran, and fell on his neck, and kissed him.
Luke 15:20 (KJV)

This poignant scene is the third in a trio of paintings. Only Luke portrays the stories of the lost sheep, the lost coin, and the lost son. These pictures touch our hearts because, as Barbara Brown Taylor, rector of Grace-Calvary Church, writes:

I am the poor, tuckered-out lamb, draped across my dear redeemer's shoulders so full of gratitude and relief that I vow never to wander away from him again. Or I am the silver coin, lying in some dark corner of the universe until the good woman who will not give up on me sweeps me into the light.[25]

Yet as comforting as it is to identify with the found in each of these illustrations, God wants us to go deeper. First, He wants us to identify with the seeker: with the shepherd who is rejoicing over his recovered lamb and with the housewife who is jumping up and down because she has found her lost coin!

Prepare Your Heart to Hear
Before each of the following six devotional times, quiet your heart and ask God to speak to you personally from His Word.

Memory Review

Review Luke 1:46-50; 9:23-25; 10:38-42 this week. Prepare to say these verses in twos when you meet for discussion.

Warm-Up

Share a time when you lost something important (pet, ring, car, child . . .) and then found it! How did you feel before and after?

Day 1: Overview

While we think of these as three parables, accurately, it is one parable with three illustrations. (Jesus told them "this parable.") Therefore, the central point is the same in each.

Read Luke 15:1-2.

1.   Describe the context of this three-pictured parable. What were the religious leaders missing?

Read Luke 15:3-32.

2. In each of these pictures, find evidence for the seeker's:

	Sheep	Coin	Son
Anguish			
Joy			

3. In each of these illustrations, the seeker responds similarly upon finding the lost. Describe the response.

What is Jesus trying to help us to understand?

Day 2: Developing Our Father's Eyes

Chuck Swindoll asks: "Remember when you first became a Christian? You would lie on your bed thinking 'Who can I tell?' That's exactly how it was for me. I was highly motivated to share my faith because I had compassion for individuals who were wandering in the darkness from which I had been so recently delivered. But so often, as our eyes have grown accustomed to the light, we forget the misery of being lost."

The most fruitful Christians evangelistically are new Christians. They remember what it is like to be lost. THEY CARE!

In addition to developing compassion, we must ask for wisdom on how to approach the lost. People are lost for different reasons. Some, like the prodigal son, have rebelled. Others, like the poor little sheep, simply don't know the right path. And then there are those who are like the lost coin, who are lost because of the carelessness of others. For years I was part of the reason that one of my family members was slow in coming to Christ. I would argue with her about issues that were not central to salvation, such as abortion or homosexuality. When I asked her forgiveness for being so obnoxious and started showing her the love of the Father, the walls came down. Respected author John Stott says: "We must struggle to listen through their ears and look through their eyes so as to grasp what prevents them from hearing the gospel and seeing Christ."[26]

4.   Who are some of the lost in your life? How might you discover what it is that is keeping them from Christ?

Personal Action Assignment

Pray for the lost in your life. Write the names God impresses on your heart in your journal. Ask God to give you compassion and wisdom. Write down any thoughts you receive.

Day 3: Grace and Ungrace

In Philip Yancey's powerful book, *What's So Amazing about Grace?* he says that in Jesus' day, "the worse a person felt about herself, the more likely she saw Jesus as a refuge."[27] Today, many who are acutely aware of their sin stay away from church because Christians make them feel worse, not better! Yancey believes that is because we are not showing grace but ungrace. We have forgotten how to show grace. We need to study the portrait of the "lovesick father."

And the son said unto him, Father, I have
sinned against heaven, and in thy sight, and
am no more worthy to be called thy son.

But the father said to his servants, Bring forth
the best robe, and put it on him; and put a
ring on his hand, and shoes on his feet.
— Luke 15:21-22 (KJV)

Read Luke 15:11-24.

5. List evidences of grace of the Father. (Give references.)

Read Luke 15:25-32.

6. List evidences of grace of the Father toward the older brother.

7. How have believers shown grace to you? Can you recall a specific time? How did it impact you?

Jim Wallis, editor of Sojourners, *says: "Evangelical Christians are big on salvation but often short on grace."[28] Grace is a most unnatural act, Philip Yancey says. We are reluctant to give grace because it is so costly. (It costs the recipient nothing but it costs the giver a great deal!) However, as costly as grace is, ungrace costs more. We imprison ourselves in a jail of icy bitterness, cutting ourselves off from those who are dearest to us and we pass on a habit of ungrace to our children and grandchildren.*

8. Look up the word *grace.* Define it. Then come up with a definition of ungrace.

9. Imagine you were painting the scene in Luke 15:25-30. How would you do it to clarify the contrast between the grace inside and the ungrace of the older brother outside?

10. Luke is full of examples of "ungrace." The Pharisees, the townspeople, even, at times, the disciples. Here are a few examples, ending with the older brother. Imagine what the cost of ungrace might have been to those they hurt and to the perpetrators themselves.

    A. Luke 6:1-11

    B. Luke 7:44-47

    C. Luke 9:51-56

    D. Luke 10:30-37

    E. Luke 15:25-32

11. As you are still before the Lord, how might you be more gracious toward the people in your life?

Day 5: Prodigals All

Prodigal means "wasteful" and there is some of the prodigal in all of us. We have rebelled against the discipline of the Father, wanting to be free and to do what we want to do with our money, time, and talent. German author Helmut Thielicke, in *The Waiting Father,* comments how rare the quiet and peaceful home is today, even among Christians, because we are not really abiding in Christ.

> *Is not Europe, is not the Christian Western world on this same road of separation from its origin and the source of its blessings?*
>
> *. . . Each age has its own peculiar "far country," and so has ours. . . . It is true that we work with the Father's capital, with our energy and ambition, our highly developed reason, our technical skills . . . all these things which the Father has given us! But we use them without him. . . . That's why what we possess explodes in our hands. . . . That's why modern man has bad dreams as soon as he is alone and has a little time for reflection. That's why he has to turn on the radio or run to the movies to divert himself. . . . He cannot be alone; he must have diversion. . . . But when he cannot and therefore must, then he is no longer free!*
>
> *. . . The repentance of the lost son is therefore not something merely negative. . . . Whenever the New Testament speaks of repentance, always the great joy is in the background. It does not say, "Repent or hell will swallow you up," but "Repent, the kingdom of heaven is at hand."*[29]

Ask yourself if Helmut Thielicke's reflections apply to you. Are there areas where you are rebelling against the discipline of the Lord? Are you seeking to divert yourself to anesthetize the pain? Come home and experience the joy!

12. We are less likely to wander away if we appreciate what we have at home.
    A. Recall the darkness! Share three ways Jesus has changed your life. If you came to Christ as a child, share three ways your life might be different had you never come to the Light.

B. Think about the times when you have been particularly close to Jesus. Recall the joy and the peace.

C. List some of the blessings in your life right now.

13. Review the memory passages. As you do,
    A. In Luke 1:46-50, describe the joy Mary had in being close to the Father.

    B. In Luke 9:23-25 describe the discipline of God and how it leads to blessing.

    C. In Luke 10:38-42, describe the blessing Mary of Bethany receives by staying close to God.

Day 6: When Someone You Love Is a Prodigal

My husband returned to our bedroom at 2 A.M. after checking on our fifteen-year-old son. Steve sat on the edge of the bed, his head between his hands.

"What is it?" I asked.

"John's gone. His bed is empty, his window is open."

We imagined, correctly, that he was out with his new friends, older boys who liked to party, boys John had met at his new job. My husband and I held each other and prayed for John.

The next six months were some of the most difficult we had ever experienced as a family. John was rebellious and moody—so different from the obedient and joyful boy we'd known for fifteen years. He suffered the consequences of some of his wrong choices, and as painful as it was, we did not try to intervene to spare him those consequences. However, we did give him love and support. (The police suspected someone in that crowd of theft— we went with John to the station where he was fingerprinted and interrogated.)

Perhaps the most helpful thing we did during that time was to try to maintain our relationship. My godly friend Shirley Ellis advised me: "Even though you are angry with John, show him you love him. If you can't talk to him, give him backrubs, play chess with him." My sister Sally fasted and prayed with me that God would protect John during his prodigal journey and bring him safely back to Himself.

One night I received a phone call from our youth pastor asking if a traveling Nebraska football player could stay at our house. When I told John that Travis Turner would be our guest, John's eyes lit up. "Travis Turner? Here? In our house?" Travis was not only well known in Nebraska for football, he loved the Lord and was responsive to His Spirit. Travis stayed up with John until the wee hours of the morning, talking to him about his walk with Christ. The next day John came to us and said: "I've sinned against God and against you. I'm going to quit my job, become active in the youth group, and find new, *godly* friends. And I'm going to memorize the Sermon on the Mount in the next three months so that I can walk the kind of walk Travis Turner walks." And John kept his word. Today, fifteen years later, John is still walking with the Lord, a godly husband and father. How I thank God for restoring our son to Himself.

14. As difficult as it is, sometimes we need to allow a child to experience the pain of wrong choices. How do you see this in the Parable of the Two Sons? (Give references.)

What are some ways a mother might allow her child to experience the pain of wrong choices?

15. As difficult as it is, we need to continue to show our children love, even if we have been hurt or disappointed by them. How do you see this in the father's attitude toward both his sons? (Give references.)

What are some ways a mother might show her prodigal child love without endorsing his wrong choices?

16. How has God allowed you to experience the pain of wrong choices?

How has He shown you love even when you disappointed Him?

17. If time permits, give an opportunity for women to share what they think they will remember from this lesson.

Extra Credit
Read Luke 16–17. What did you learn?

Prayer Time
Pair in twos. Have a time of thanksgiving for ways God has shown grace to you. Confess silently or audibly ways you have rebelled at God's discipline. Then pray for lost loved ones. Close with Psalm 51:10-13.

the Fourth Oasis

THE SAVIOR'S VICTORY

Some of our women amazed us.
They went to the tomb early this
morning but didn't find His body.
They came and told us that they
had seen a vision of angels,
who said He was alive.
—Luke 24:22-23

The Savior's Victory

Luke 22–24

Dark events swirl around the Savior in Luke 22 and 23. Luke makes it clear this is a spiritual battle. C.S. Lewis captured the drama of this spiritual battle in his allegory, *The Lion, the Witch, and the Wardrobe.* Lucy and Susan sense that something dreadful is about to happen and crouch behind the bushes. They watch a spiritual battle between Aslan and the witch's army of ogres, hags, cruels, ettins . . . Aslan's great mane is sheared, his jaw muzzled, and he is tied to a stone table.

> *Then the ogre stood back and the children, watching from their hiding place, could see the face of Aslan looking all small and different without its mane. The enemies also saw the difference.*
>
> *"Why, he's only a great cat after all!" cried one.*
>
> *. . . And they surged round Aslan, jeering at him, saying things like "Puss, Puss! Poor Pussy. . . . "*

The children wait for Aslan's roar to spring upon his enemies, but it doesn't happen. Instead, the witch draws near:

> *She stood by Aslan's head. Her face was working and twitching with passion, but he looked up at the sky, still quiet, neither angry nor afraid, but a little sad. Then, just before she gave the blow, she stooped down and said in a quivering voice,*

"And now, who has won? Fool, did you think that by all this you would save the human traitor? Now I will kill you instead of him as our pact was and so the Deep Magic will be appeased. . . . "

The children did not see the actual moment of the killing. They couldn't bear to look and had covered their eyes.

The witch has magic, but Aslan has deeper magic, magic that has existed, Lewis says, from "before the dawn of time." Days later:

There, shining in the sunrise, larger than they had seen him before, shaking his mane (for it had apparently grown again) stood Aslan himself.

. . . "You're not—not a—?" asked Susan in a shaky voice. She couldn't bring herself to say the word ghost. Aslan stooped his golden head and licked her forehead. The warmth of his breath and a rich sort of smell that seemed to hang about his hair came all over her.

"Do I look it?" he said.

"Oh, you're real, you're real! Oh, Aslan!" cried Lucy, and both girls flung themselves upon him and covered him with kisses.[30]

Satan *is* powerful, and you will see that he put up a tremendous fight here to destroy Jesus. Yet, killing Jesus, says Walter Wink, was like trying to destroy a dandelion seed-head by blowing on it.[31]

Extra Credit
Read Luke 18:15–21:19. What stood out to you?

Tenth Stop!
The Savior's Farewell

ave you ever moved away from friends and family? Or felt the pain of a child leaving for college, marriage, or the mission field? Some of the most poignant words written are about such parting scenes. Shakespeare said, "Parting is such sweet sorrow." Amy Carmichael writes of "the rending" between her and the man who had become like a father to her when she felt the call to the mission field in China. She felt she would break his heart if she left him, but the call was clear. She stood at the rail of the ship, looking at his dear wrinkled face, perhaps, she thought, for the last time. Fifty-two years later she wrote:

> *Never, I think, not even in Heaven shall I forget that parting. It was such a rending thing that I never wanted to repeat it. . . . Even now my heart winces at the thought of it. The night I sailed for China, March 3, 1893, my life, on the human side was broken, and it never was mended again.*[32]

This was the intense emotion Jesus was feeling. John tells us Jesus "loved them unto the end" (John 13:1, KJV). Luke tells us He "earnestly" desired to eat this Passover with them (Luke 22:15). Literally, He says, "With desire I have desired," reflecting the intensity. It is as if one were to have a last Christmas Eve with those who were the very dearest on earth to her before she was to die on Christmas Day.

Prepare Your Heart to Hear
Father, help me put myself in the place of those to whom this actually happened. Make it live for me.

Memory Work

In this victory oasis you will memorize Luke 23:28; 24:38-39.

> **Jesus turned and said to them, "Daughters of Jerusalem, do not weep for Me; weep for yourselves and for your children" (Luke 23:28).**

Warm-Up

Describe a parting scene you have witnessed or experienced. What were the emotions?

Day 1: Overview

Dr. Darrell Bock writes:

> *Sinister forces are behind Jesus' death. . . . the events surrounding Jesus' ministry are part of a larger, cosmic drama between great spiritual powers. Heaven and hell are interested in the fate of Jesus. In the great chess match, this is Satan's major move to remove Jesus from the game.*[33]

1. Read all of the introductory notes. Comment on what stood out to you from:
   A. The Introductory notes for THE FOURTH OASIS: THE SAVIOR'S VICTORY (pp. 120–121)

In what ways does C.S. Lewis communicate that the battle was a spiritual battle with dark forces?

B. The Introductory notes for THE TENTH STOP! THE SAVIOR'S FAREWELL (p. 122)

Read Luke 22 as an overview.

2.   Find evidence for the fact that this is a spiritual battle, but Jesus is in control. (Give verse references.)

Spend five minutes on the memory passage.

Journal Entry: What did God impress on your heart? Make a brief entry in your journal.

Day 2: Meaningful Meals and Celebrations

For us as Christians, Christmas, Easter, and Thanksgiving are our most important and festive holidays. For the Jews, the most important holiday time was Passover. As with us, this time was set apart for remembering, for showing love to family, and for celebrating with feasting, music, and tradition!

For us as women, holidays are important, because we often are the ones who seize them as an opportunity to show love. Likewise, meals are important to us, because we are often the ones preparing them, longing to make them vessels of love. Intriguingly, holidays, celebrations, and meals are important in Luke, perhaps because one of his primary sources was women.

Here, in Luke 22, Jesus prepares to celebrate the Passover meal with His loved ones. Today we will look at the significance of meals in Luke, and of celebrations, and of seizing them to glorify God and to show love. Tomorrow we will look at why Passover was the time that God chose to have the Savior die.

3.   Meals should be a way of showing love, of celebrating God's goodness, or of being a catalyst for intimate conversation. How can you see this in the following passages?

A. Luke 9:13-17

B. Luke 14:12-14

C. Luke 15:22-24

4.   Meals, as God intended, should be a time of showing love. But they can be ruined. In a phrase, what was lacking in each of the following scenes?
     A. What did Simon the Pharisee lack? (Luke 7:44-47)

     B. What did Martha lack? (Luke 11:38-42)

     C. What did those invited lack? (Luke 14:15-24)

     D. What did the older brother lack? (Luke 15:25-30)

5.   What can a woman do to increase the chances that there will be a spirit of love and graciousness at family meals?

What can a woman do to facilitate meaningful conversation at meals shared with family or friends?

If, on Christmas Day, you suspected that it would be your last, the day would be particularly poignant. Harold Shaw experienced this when he had lung cancer. In God in the Dark Luci Shaw describes some of the emotions that she saw in her husband on that Christmas Day. I think Jesus had similar feelings the night of His last Passover Supper.

> *Christmas Day. Bright, clear, minus three degrees. . . . We opened presents, and I took lots of photographs. . . .*
>
> *After baked ham, we had cake in the family room. It seemed natural to suggest that we all pray for Harold. "But first," he said, "I want to read you some of the Bible passages that have come alive for me in the last few weeks." Harold is a good reader, but he struggled with the words and his emotions as he read. Then he prayed for each of us in the room, for the future mates of John, Jeff, and Kris, and for all our grandchildren, born and yet to be born, blessing us all in the name of Christ.*
>
> *One by one, each of us was crying, out of our grief and incredulity, our sense of loss, pain, and fear. Kris lay sobbing on the couch, her feet in H.'s lap and her head in Marian's lap. It was a good, hard, precious, difficult, close, intense, unifying time. . . .*[34]

6. What would be some of the things you would want to do if you were spending your last Christmas with your loved ones?

Why might it be wise to create an opportunity for your loved ones to express their feelings for each other at the next holiday gathering? How might you facilitate that opportunity?

In our family we often have a time of "blessing" each other by having each person share specific reasons why they are thankful for the person on their right or left. Or, if the gathering is a smaller holiday gathering, we each bless each guest.

Group Action Assignment
Plan a meal together at which you will bless one another!

7. At the meal in Luke 22:24-32, find an instance when:
    A. Jesus instructs them

    B. Jesus thanks or blesses them

    C. Jesus warns, encourages, and instructs Simon

Day 3: I Have Eagerly Desired to Eat This Passover with You
The Passover meal was the most important of the Jewish feasts, a time when the nation reflected on its deliverance. It was no coincidence that Jesus, our Passover Lamb, died at this time. God planned the year, the day, and the hour. The Passover lambs were sacrificed on the fourteenth day of the month of Nisan between the hours of 2:30 and 5:30 P.M. That is precisely the time when Jesus, our perfect Lamb of God, died.

And Jesus knew. He knew He would not be there to eat the Passover meal with His beloved disciples. Therefore, He planned to eat it with them early, on the thirteenth day of the month of Nisan.

H.D.M. Spence explains a threefold purpose for the intense longing of Jesus to celebrate this last Passover with His disciples. He longs to bid them farewell, as we would with our loved ones if we knew we were dying tomorrow. He longs to instruct them. And He longs, as the Founder of the one true religion, to transform the Passover feast of deliverance into a supper which will commemorate a far greater deliverance.[35]

8. Read Exodus 12:1-30 and answer the following:
   A. What were the Israelites instructed to do in verses 5-7?

   B. What parallel do you see with Christ?

   C. Why were they to continue to observe this supper every year? (verses 24-28)

   D. Not only were the Israelites delivered from death, but from slavery. Is there an "enslaving" habit (anger, gluttony . . .) from which Christ's power has set you free?

Personal Action Assignment
Is there a sin that is still enslaving you? Fall to your knees and ask Jesus to deliver you from that spirit of addiction and to replace it with a spirit of joy and peace.

Read Luke 22:7-20.

9. At what point does Jesus transform the Passover meal into a supper which will commemorate a far greater deliverance?

When we take Communion, we can look backward to Passover, and forward to an even greater meal (verse 18). What is it? (See Revelation 19:9.)

Day 4: Satan Entered Judas

In *The Screwtape Letters,* C.S. Lewis says, "There are two equal and opposite errors into which our race can fall about the devils. One is to disbelieve in their existence. The other is to believe, and to feel an excessive and unhealthy interest in them."[36]

Certainly Luke 22 makes it clear Satan is real, and that we had better be alert!

Read Luke 22:1-7.

10. Why was Jerusalem so crowded, and why did this present a difficulty for the chief priests and officers of the temple guard? (Compare Luke 19:47-48.)

How did Judas help them with their dilemma? Why do you think they rejoiced?

11. What lies might Satan have possibly whispered to Judas to tempt the betrayal?

12. Judas certainly stands as a warning that proximity to Jesus and His followers is not enough—Jesus wants our hearts! What warning does Jesus give in Luke 6:43-49?

13. It is easy to deceive ourselves and think we are obeying when we are really just hearing. How do we know? By fruit. Examine the following branches of your life and see if there is consistently good fruit:

A. Relationships (husband, in-laws, friends, family, other)

B. Habits (quiet time, eating, housekeeping, other)

C. Compassion (the unsaved, the hungry, the hurting)

Read Luke 22:21-23.

14. Though Jesus' death is destined, still, Judas is personally responsible for the betrayal. How does Jesus express this here?

What else does Jesus tell us in Matthew 26:24? What does this mean?

How does Judas show his hypocrisy in Matthew 26:25?

15. How does Judas show his hypocrisy in Luke 22:47-48?

16. Hypocrisy is a sin that tempts us when we long for the praise of men instead of the praise of God, when we are building our own little kingdom instead of the kingdom of God. Show how this is true in the following:

    A. Luke 11:37-42

    B. Luke 20:46-47

17. Do you long for the praise of men or of God?

    Which is wiser? Why?

Review your memory verse.

Personal Action Assignment

Pray for protection for yourself and your loved ones. Pray that you will desire the praise of God, and not of men, for one of Satan's frequent lures is the praise of men. (See Luke 4:5-7.)

Day 5: Simon, Simon, Satan Has Asked to Sift You

When we are strong, we are dangerous in Satan's eyes. Peter was bold—he was the leader. Ken Gire, in *Intimate Moments with the Savior,* describes it like this:

> *Satan wants to thresh his faith and beat it into the ground until the husk breaks open. Then he'll show the world what's really inside Peter's heart. And once the other disciples see this, the backbone of the revolution will be as good as crushed.*[37]

18. Summarize the following passages:
    A. Luke 22:31-32

    B. Luke 22:33-34

    C. Luke 22:54-62

    D. John 21:15-19

    E. Matthew 27:1-5

19. Judas was lost, but Peter reinstated. Both were sad about their sin, so what do you think made the difference? (See 2 Corinthians 7:9-10.)

Day 6: Jesus' Response to Those Who Hurt Him

How do you respond when you have given and given to someone and then they hurt you?

Most of us withdraw. We think: "How could she do this? If she really loved me, if she really appreciated all I have done for her, then she wouldn't have hurt me." And yet, if we are honest, we know that we have hurt people we love deeply.

Jesus kept on loving. Jesus gave grace.

20. Describe how Jesus responds to those who hurt Him:
    A. Luke 22:42

    B. Luke 22:45-46

    C. Luke 22:47-48

    D. Luke 22:49-51

    E. Luke 24:34

21. Describe one time when you have let Jesus down. How did He respond?

What does God ask of us in Ephesians 4:32?

22. How has God spoken to you through this lesson?

Prayer Time

Instead of sharing individual prayer requests, have each woman lift her own request up in prayer. Then have a few women support her with sentences. When there is a silence, another woman should lift up her individual prayer request.

Eleventh Stop!
Do Not Weep for Me

 hroughout his Gospel Luke emphasizes:

Jesus is the Christ sent for all *people!*

Remember what the angel said at the beginning of Luke's Gospel? Good news for all people! Yet not all will receive this good news. Here, at the end of Jesus' earthly life, you will see a wide spectrum of responses to Him.

You cannot remain neutral, though you may try, as Pilate did, but ultimately you will be held accountable for your failure to totally embrace Him. Whether you are a man or a woman, Jew or Gentile, rich or poor—indifference is as dangerous as opposition. Judgment awaits those who are hard or soft in their rejection of the Christ. Max Lucado says: "As long as you can take him or leave him, you might as well leave him, because he won't be taken halfheartedly."[38]

This man, despised and broken, is the Messiah. Dr. Darrell Bock says: "If there is one thing that Luke is after in his Gospel, it is the need to totally embrace the Innocent One who died."[39] If you have not embraced Jesus, take the following words of Jesus to heart:

Daughters of Jerusalem, do not weep for Me; weep for yourselves and for your children.   Luke 23:28

Prepare Your Heart to Hear
Each day, before you begin, ask God to speak personally to you. Write what impresses you in your journal.

Memory Work

Review Luke 23:28. During the next two weeks complete:

> He said to them, "Why are you troubled, and why do doubts rise in your minds? Look at My hands and My feet. It is I Myself! Touch Me and see; a ghost does not have flesh and bones, as you see I have." Luke 24:38-39

Warm-Up

Call out some words which describe responses you have seen to Jesus. What do you think is the most common?

Day 1: Overview—Part I

The death and resurrection of Jesus shows us He was much more than a great moral teacher. Yet that is how many in the world define Him. Perhaps they do so out of ignorance, or perhaps, like Pilate, they are trying to be positive toward Jesus without wholeheartedly embracing Him. However, this response is not logical. In *Mere Christianity* C.S. Lewis explains:

> *A man who was merely a man and said the sort of things Jesus said would not be a great moral teacher. He would either be a lunatic—on a level with the man who says he is a poached egg—or else he would be the Devil of Hell.*[40]

Lewis puts this in allegory form in *The Lion, the Witch, and the Wardrobe.* Lucy has come out of the wardrobe with a fantastic story about discovering another world—and her siblings dismiss her story as preposterous. The professor responds:

> *"Logic!" said the Professor half to himself. "Why don't they teach logic at these schools? There are only three possibilities. Either your sister is telling lies, or she is mad, or she is telling the truth. You know she doesn't tell lies and it is obvious that she is not mad. For the moment then and unless any further evidence turns up, we must assume that she is telling the truth."*[41]

1.   What stood out to you from the Introduction for THE ELEVENTH STOP! DO NOT WEEP FOR ME (p. 135)

2. What stood out to you from the Introduction for Day 1 (p. 136)?

Read Luke 22:63 through Luke 23:31.

3.   Describe *who* responded to Jesus and *how.* Note also any response of Jesus in return.
     A. Luke 22:63-65

     B. Luke 22:66-71

     C. Luke 23:1-7

     D. Luke 23:8-11

     E. Luke 23:13-25

F. Luke 23:27

4. Summarize the above negative responses to Jesus. What impresses you about the way Jesus responds? Sing "When I Survey the Wonderous Cross" from your hymnal. Learn your memory passage.

Day 2: Overview—Part II
He could have called ten thousand, but He chose to die for you and me.

5. Describe who responded to Jesus and how.

A. Luke 23:35-37

B. Luke 23:39

C. Luke 23:40-43

D. Luke 23:47

E. Luke 23:50-53

F. Luke 23:55-56

6. Which of the above responded positively to Jesus? How does Luke show by this that the good news is for all people?

Spend five minutes on your memory passage.

Sing "Hallelujah, What a Savior!" from your hymnal.

Day 3: Herod and Pilate Became Friends

What made friends of two former enemies? Their rejection of Christ! Their rejection was different: Herod mocked Christ and Pilate tried to wash his hands of Him (Matthew 27:24), but the result was the same. They rejected the Innocent One God had sent and they will be judged.

It's intriguing to trace the response of Pilate to Jesus. He had many warnings. Even his wife warned him:

While Pilate was sitting on the judge's seat, his wife sent him this message: "Don't have anything to do with that innocent man, for I have suffered a great deal today in a dream because of Him." Matthew 27:19

Pilate did what he did out of fear. It's helpful to know that Pilate's predecessor was put to death for falling out of grace with his political superior, Caesar. See how the crowd preys upon Pilate's fear of Caesar.

7. What does the crowd tell Pilate in Luke 23:1-2?

Was it true that Jesus opposed paying taxes? (See Luke 20:20-26)

How does Jesus respond to the charge of being King of the Jews?

8. What other details does John give us concerning the reply of Jesus to Pilate in John 18:36-37?

What enigmatic reply does Pilate make to this in John 18:38a?

9. How does Pilate try to escape judging Jesus? (Luke 23:6-7)

Is he successful? (Luke 23:11)

10. When Jesus comes back to Pilate, how does Pilate try to appease the crowd? (Luke 23:16)

Pilate keeps trying to wriggle out of his corner. The other Gospel writers give us more detail here.

11. Describe what happens in Matthew 27:21-26.

12. In John 19:7-16 describe:
    A. Pilate's fear (John 19:8)

    B. Jesus' response (John 19:11)

Contrary to what many evangelicals believe, there are degrees of sin. Pilate was sinning, and he would be held guilty, but in John 19:11 Jesus tells Pilate that the one who handed him over to Pilate was guilty of the greater sin. However, the guilt of others will not acquit us on Judgment Day. Matthew Henry says that it will not "avail in the great day to say others were worse than we. . . . [42]

13. Fearing man or God:
    A. What method finally gives the crowd success with Pilate in John 19:12?

    B. How does the thief on the cross show greater wisdom than Pilate? (Luke 23:40a)

    C. What does Jesus tell us in Luke 12:5?

    D. Give some situations in which your fear of man might keep you from doing what is best.

Day 4: Daughters of Jerusalem

The term "Daughters of Jerusalem" or "Daughters of Zion" (Zion is interchangeable with Jerusalem as Zion is the mountain on which Jerusalem is built) refers to the daughters which live in that city. When the phrase is singular ("Daughter of

Jerusalem") it means the city, for cities, though they include males and females, are usually considered feminine. However, when it is written in the plural ("Daughters of Jerusalem"), it seems to be directed toward just the women. This happens in three different books: Isaiah, Song of Songs, and Luke.

In Song of Songs, the "Daughters of Jerusalem" are continually asking questions of the bride, as they are enthralled and curious about her love for her lover and his love for her. (When our daughter Sally was married she and her groom, Jeremie, designed their wedding around the Song of Songs. Instead of bridesmaids and groomsmen they had "Daughters and Sons of Jerusalem" who asked them, in chorus, about their love for each other and their love for God.) Many commentators believe that the Song of Songs, in addition to being a portrait of the beauty of married love, is also a reflection of the beauty of the love between Christ and His bride, the true church. It seems to me that in the Song of Songs the Daughters of Jerusalem are curious and enchanted, but do not necessarily embrace Christ themselves. It is possible to be enchanted by religion; by Christmas carols, midnight mass, stained-glass windows, and angels and yet, miss Jesus.

In Isaiah, the Daughters of Zion were far from God, even though they lived right in Jerusalem. Simply being close to the truth, being the daughter of a pastor, raised in the church, or living in a spiritual mecca like Wheaton, Colorado Springs, or Jerusalem does not mean that you know Jesus. God is holy and He will punish sin. We all need to repent, embrace the Savior, and bear fruit worthy of repentance.

In the New Testament, the term "Daughters of Jerusalem" occurs only in Luke. Here, again, though the women are not hostile to Jesus, they have missed the truth. Seeing His torn flesh and bleeding brow, they sympathize with His suffering. But Jesus turns to them and says: "Weep not for Me, weep for yourselves." There are many today who consider themselves believers, yet, they have not mourned for their own sin and turned around to wholeheartedly embrace Jesus as Lord. Dr. Darrell Bock says: "Not all opposition to Jesus is hard opposition."[43]

14. Summarize what you learned from the above about the "Daughters of Jerusalem."

What stood out to you personally? Why?

15. Describe the "Daughters" in the following passages. These women were missing something important. Explain what you see.
   A. Isaiah 3:16-34

   B. Luke 23:27-28

God's love and protection for women should not lull us into complacency, into the false belief that only men will be held accountable for living wholeheartedly for Christ. Jesus certainly makes this clear in His exhortation to the Daughters of Jerusalem. It isn't enough for women to hear God's Word (Luke 8:21), nor is it enough to feel emotion about God, as the Daughters of Jerusalem did. We must wake up and walk in the light all day long.

16. Is His spirit speaking to you in any way from the above? If so, how?

Review your memory work of Luke 23:27.

Sing "Living for Jesus" from your hymnal.

Day 5: Judgment

In the passages you will study today you will read of judgment. When the prophets, including Jesus, talked about judgment it usually referred to both a near and a distant judgment. Jesus warns of the fall of Jerusalem, which did occur in A.D. 70 It was just as Jesus prophesied here and in Luke 20. Jerusalem was surrounded. Women and little children were victims as well. The terror was great. There is a pattern, for one day the terror of the final judgment will be great.

17. Have you ever personally experienced a natural disaster such as an earthquake, a flood, or a tornado? If so, share some of your feelings, or what you imagine your feelings would be.

18. Why does Jesus weep over Jerusalem in the following passages? What phrases reveal His compassion?
    A. Luke 13:34-35

    B. Luke 19:41-44

    C. Luke 21:20-24

Prophecy is meant to warn us. When the Roman armies were gathering in A.D. 70, the Christian congregations remembered the words of Jesus spoken here and fled to Pella beyond Jordan.[44] May we, likewise, believe God's warning of the coming judgment and become, not just good women, but excellent and pure women of God. Jesus continues now with a distant prophecy, showing God's pattern in judgment.

19. In Luke 21:25-36
    A. What will be the cosmic signs that the end is near? (verse 25)

    B. How will people respond? (verse 26)

C. How will Jesus arrive? (verse 27)

D. How should we respond to this warning? (verses 34-36)

20. Why were the people in charge of the *Titanic,* and also of the *Challenger,* complacent? What warnings did they ignore? What proper precautions did they fail to take?

Why are people, even believers, complacent about the coming judgment? What warnings (21:34-35) are they ignoring? What proper precautions are they failing to take? (21:36)

21. In order to become an excellent and pure woman of God who will be unashamed when Jesus returns, what do you need to do (or continue doing)? Are you preparing those around you for when Jesus returns?

Review your memory work.

In your personal devotional time sing "And Can It Be?"

Day 6: Responding in Faith
Luke has shown us a variety of negative responses to Jesus, some hard, some soft, but all resulting in judgment. There is the hard rejection of the religious leaders, the frivolity of Herod, spinelessness of Pilate, and the misdirected

weeping of the Daughters of Jerusalem.

Now Luke closes his passion account with responses of faith.

22. Although the thief on the cross did not utter a traditional "sinner's prayer," his response brought him forgiveness. What do you see in his response? What do you learn from Jesus' words? (Luke 23:40-43)

23. How did the centurion respond? (Luke 23:47) Review Luke 23 and record what the centurion might have witnessed that led him to his response of faith.

24. Luke describes certain people as good and righteous, among them Zechariah, Elizabeth, Simeon, Anna, and now, Joseph of Arimathea. What did Joseph of Arimathea do? What does this tell you about him? (Luke 23:50-54)

John 19:39 tells us that Nicodemus helped Joseph and that they anointed Him with seventy-five pounds of spices, the amount usually reserved for a king.[45]

25. What do you see that is commendable in the women who had come with Jesus? (Luke 23:55-56)

Contrast their response to the disciples. To the Daughters of Jerusalem.

26. What do you think you will remember from this lesson?

How could you apply it to your life?

Prayer Time

Pray first for urgent needs. Then spend time in prayer for each other to become pure and excellent women of God. In groups of four or five, choose a leader who will lift up the name of each woman in your circle to God. Then whoever feels prompted should lift up a short sentence prayer for that woman. When there is a silence, the leader should lift up the name of the next woman. Some Scriptures that might guide you in praying for each other are: Philippians 1:9-11 and Titus 2:3-5.

Last Stop!
A Slow Dawning

*I*t has the ring of truth. Instead of confidently believing, they grope about in half-light, slowly coming to the truth, like the dim-witted creatures we all truly are.

The women:
>   They wonder . . .
>   They are frightened, yet filled with joy . . .
>   Then they remember His words . . .

The disciples:
>   The women's words seem like nonsense.
>   Peter saw the strips of linen lying by themselves . . . he went away, wondering . . .

I love the escalating drama. Luke alone paints the beautiful portrait of the two on the road to Emmaus. Here again, they are puzzled, confused, even angry! There is humor as Jesus joins them and they do not recognize Him. Instead, they vent their emotions. And He shares from the Word with them, widening their light, causing their hearts to burn within them. And then, when He dines with them, their eyes are opened! They see!

Oh, can it be? Yes! He is risen! HE IS RISEN INDEED!

Prepare Your Heart to Hear
Each day, ask God to help you recognize Him, as He did for the two on the road to Emmaus!

Memory Work
Complete Luke 24:38-39:

> **He said to them, "Why are you troubled, and why do doubts rise in your minds? Look at My hands and My feet. It is I Myself! Touch Me and see; a ghost does not have flesh and bones, as you see I have."**

Warm-Up
Think about the dearest person to you on earth. Imagine he (or she) died cruelly and unexpectedly. And then, on the third day, you heard he was alive. How do you think you would react? Why?

Day 1: Overview
In *The Jesus I Never Knew* Philip Yancey says "the crowd challenged Jesus to prove himself by climbing down from the cross, but not one person thought of what actually would happen: that he would die and come back." The surprise that morning is great. "Accounts of the empty tomb sound breathless and fragmentary. . . . Surely conspirators could have done a neater job of depicting what they would later claim to be a huge hinge of history . . . unless of course they were not concocting a legend but recording the plain facts."[46]

Read Luke 24.

1.   As you read, observe the confusion, the bewilderment, the slowly dawning light. Find examples like the one given:

Who	What	Why
women	wondering	the stone rolled away and the body gone

Review your memory work.

Day 2: Resurrection Discovered

Of all the major religions, only Christianity values women. All through His life Jesus defied the culture and reached out to women, shocking the men around Him. Historian Flavius Josephus reflects the prejudice of the day when he writes: "Let not the testimony of women be admitted, on account of the levity and boldness of their sex."[47] All four Gospel writers record women as being the first at the empty tomb! Philip Yancy says no conspirator in the first century would have invented *that!* But the truth is, God allowed women to be there first, to be the first to see Jesus, to be the first to tell the amazing story.[48]

Read Luke 24:1-12.

2. Why do you think God allowed women to be at the tomb first?

   As a woman, what does this mean to you?

3. While the women were wondering about the missing body, what happened? Describe what they saw and heard.

4. How was the third day the day of salvation in these passages?
   A. Genesis 22:4

   B. Genesis 42:17-18

C. Esther 5:1

D. Hosea 6:2

E. Jonah 1:17

F. Luke 24:7, 21, 45

5.   What significance do you see in the above pattern?

6.   The women reported *everything*. What would that include? How did the apostles respond?

The "nonsense" is a word used in medical settings of the delirious talk of the very ill![49]

Day 3: We Had Hoped Jesus Was the One!
This beautiful story, told in detail by Luke alone, is filled with suspense, drama, and humor. Cleopas and another believer are on the road to Emmaus, sharing their confusion and disappointment, when Jesus joins them. They do not recognize Him, but pour out their disappointment to Him. Walter Wangerin imagines it like this:

. . . As soon as Cleopas glanced at him, the stranger said, "Friends, what are you talking about?"

All at once Cleopas' daughter stopped and put her head down and began to cry. Until that moment it had not occurred to him that she would be as sorrowful as he. . . . Cleopas, hearing such despair in his young daughter, suddenly realized who he was angry at.

"This morning an idiot woman told us that the grave was empty and that Jesus was alive," he said. "Simon went and looked. They were right. The grave was empty. But that means absolutely nothing. And he who caused us to hope has now become the death of hope! Jesus, Teacher, Messiah pah! That is what that dead man taught me: to hate life because everything is vanity and nothing is more than a striving after wind!"

Cleopas was furious with Jesus.

"Ah, you foolish fellow," the stranger said, "slow to believe what the prophets have spoken!"

If his daughter hadn't put her arms around him and held him so tightly, Cleopas would have hit the man.

Softly, earnestly, she asked, "What did the prophets say?"[50]

Read Luke 24:13-35.

7.   In this story, what emotions do you see? (Give references.) Look carefully at the scriptural text and also try to identify with the characters. *Why* do you think they would be feeling what they seemed to be feeling in each case?

8.   What did Jesus do in both Luke 24:27 and 24:44-45?

What caused you to place your trust in Christ? One of the evidences that per-suaded my sister Sally was the change in the apostles from a ragged band who were hiding out to a fearless army, willing to be martyred for the truth. For me, it was, in part, the prophecies. I can identify with the two on the road to Emmaus, whose hearts burned within them as Jesus opened the Scriptures to them! But it is also clear that we recognized Jesus because He opened our eyes.

9. What common theme do you see in the following?
    A. Luke 9:45

    B. Luke 18:34

    C. Luke 24:16

    D. Luke 24:31

Day 4: Were Not Our Hearts Burning within Us?

How exciting it must have been to be these two disciples. Which Scriptures from Moses, the Psalms, and the Prophets did Jesus show them? Wouldn't you love to know? I would!

Dr. Darrell Bock told me we may have a clue because the early sermons by the apostles, as recorded by Luke in Acts, are laced with Scriptures from Moses, the Psalms, and the Prophets! As you look at them, ask God to open your eyes, the way He did for the two on the road to Emmaus! (Turn in your hymnal and sing: "Open My Eyes That I May See.")

10. Look carefully at each of these verses in Acts *(and the context)* and then look at its original source. On the basis of what the apostles are saying, how do you think Jesus might have explained these Old Testament Scriptures to their fellow believers on the road to Emmaus?

A. Acts 3:22 (Deuteronomy 18:15)
Dr. Bock thinks Jesus may have begun with this verse. Why would this be a logical starting place?

B. Acts 4:11 (Psalm 118:22)

C. Acts 4:25-26 (Psalm 2:1-2)

D. Acts 2:34-35 (Psalm 110:1)
This psalm is quoted extensively in the New Testament. It affirms the Deity of Jesus and His eternal priesthood.

E. Acts 2:17 (Joel 2:28-32)

F. Acts 13:33 (Psalm 2:7)

G. Acts 13:35 (Psalm 16:10)

H. Acts 13:47 (Isaiah 49:6)

11. What truths impressed you from the above questions?

Day 5: A Ghost Has Not Flesh and Bones

In Billy Graham's autobiography, *Just As I Am,* he tells of a man coming to his wife's door and claiming to be Jesus. '"Well," Ruth responded, "why did you have to knock? Why didn't you just come in through the closed door?" He stopped and scratched his head, then got back in his car and drove down the mountain.[51]

Can you imagine how the disciples felt when Jesus suddenly stood among them? (John tells us the door was locked!) The disciples thought they were seeing a ghost! And Jesus read their minds and reassured them by letting them touch Him, by watching Him eat!

Read Luke 24:36-49.

12. Describe the feelings you think the disciples had and why.

13. In the following passages, how do you see John and Peter reflecting back to these days?
A. 2 Peter 1:16

B. 1 John 1:1-3

14. What commission does Jesus give them in Luke 24:46-49?

The disciples are not abandoned but commissioned. In a world where many do not know their place, identity, or purpose, the resurrection means that disciples can know that God is at work, that Jesus is alive in glory, and that death is not the end.

Darrell Bock[52]

15. Describe the Ascension in Luke 24:50-53. Imagine being there. What would be your feelings?

16. How is your life different because of the events described in Luke 24?

In your personal quiet time sing "Because He Lives" from your hymnal and spend some time giving thanks to Him.

Day 6: The Take-Away

At the first writing seminar I attended, I was asked: "What will be the "take-away" from your book? The "take-away" is what the reader will remember from a book long after she has closed the cover.

Certain themes prevailed in Luke's Gospel, themes which he wanted you to take away! In answering these questions, be a ponderer, like Mary the mother of Jesus, like Mary of Bethany. You may very well double the impact of this study on your life by the value you place on this final day.

17. Luke wanted you to know WHO Jesus is. Find several key scenes from Luke that proclaim or show the identity of Jesus.

18. Luke wanted you to know that Jesus came for ALL people. Give examples of each from Luke. Find several key scenes to show Jesus came for Jews, for Gentiles, for women, and for children.

19. Luke wanted you to know how you fit into God's plan. The plan for believers begins in Luke and continues in Acts. (Once Luke and Acts were one book.) Being attentive to God's Spirit and responding in faith are crucial. Recall a few women who exemplified this. What did they do that made them stand out? Be specific, for this is key for your life.

20. Review your notes and summarize your take-away for:
THE FIRST OASIS: THE SAVIOR'S BIRTH

THE SECOND OASIS: THE SAVIOR'S POWER

THE THIRD OASIS: THE SAVIOR'S WISDOM

THE FOURTH OASIS: THE SAVIOR'S VICTORY

Prayer Time
Write down two ways you would like to grow in godliness. Share those and then pray for one another in this regard!

Sources

The First Oasis: The Savior's Birth

1. Darrell L. Bock, *Luke,* Vol. 1. 1:1–9:50 (Grand Rapids: Baker, 1994), 111.
2. Luci Shaw, "Yes to Shame and Glory," *Christianity Today.* Dec. 1986, 22.
3. Walter Wangerin, Jr., *The Book of God: The Bible as a Novel* (Grand Rapids: Zondervan, 1996), 580–81.
4. R.M. Edgar, "Luke." *The Pulpit Commentary,* Vol. 16. Ed. H.D.M. Spence and Joseph S. Excell (Peabody, Mass.: Hendrickson, n.d.), 35.
5. Dee Brestin, *The Friendships of Women* (Colorado Springs: Chariot Victor, 1997), 164.
6. W. Clarkson, "Luke." *The Pulpit Commentary,* 54.
7. Philip Yancey, *The Jesus I Never Knew* (Grand Rapids: Zondervan, 1995), 43.
8. Amy Carmichael, *Candles in the Dark* (Fort Washington, Pa.: Christian Literature Crusade, 1982), 52.
9. Evelyn Bence, *Mary's Journal: A Mother's Story* (New York: Harper, 1992), 139–41.

The Second Oasis: The Savior's Power

10. Philip Yancey, *The Jesus I Never Knew,* 21.
11. Francis A. Schaeffer, *The Church at the End of the Twentieth Century* (Downers Grove, Ill.: InterVarsity, 1970), 138–39.
12. Darrell L. Bock, *Luke,* Vol. 1. 713–14.
13. Ken Gire, *Intimate Moments with the Savior: Learning to Love* (Grand Rapids: Zondervan, 1989), 48–49.

The Third Oasis: The Savior's Wisdom

14. Dorothy Sayers, as quoted by Philip Yancey, *The Jesus I Never Knew,* 154.
15. Dr. S. Conway, "The Psalms." *The Pulpit Commentary.* Vol. 8, 255.
16. Josh Harris, "Thanks Mom and Dad," *New Attitude.* Vol. 4, No. 4, n.d., 39.
17. Walter Wangerin, Jr., *The Book of God: The Bible as a Novel,* 741–42.
18. Charles Swindoll, "Insight for Living," n.d.
19. Elwood McQuaid, *Come, Walk with Me* (Bellmawr, N.J.: Friends of Israel, 1990), 27.
20. Frederica Mathewes-Green, "Compassion," *Virtue,* March/April 1997.
21. Billy Graham, *Just As I Am: The Autobiography of Billy Graham* (New York: Harper Collins, 1997), n.p.
22. Darrell L. Bock, *Luke.* Vol. 2, 9:51–24:53 (Grand Rapids: Baker, 1996), 1063.
23. Alan Redpath, *Victorious Christian Service* (Westwood, N.J.: Revell, 1958), 23.
24. Cyril J. Barber, *Nehemiah and the Dynamics of Effective Leadership* (Neptune, N.J.: Loizeaux Brothers, 1991), 19.

25. Barbara Brown Taylor, *The Preaching Life* (Cambridge, Mass.: Cowley, 1993), 147–48.

26. John Stott, *Christian Mission in the Modern World* (Downers Grove, Ill.: InterVarsity, 1975), 81.

27. Philip Yancey, *What's So Amazing about Grace?* (Grand Rapids: Zondervan, 1997), 11.

28. Jim Wallis, as quoted in Philip Yancey, *What's So Amazing about Grace?* 2.

29. Helmut Thielicke, *The Waiting Father*, trans. by John W. Doberstein (New York: Harper, 1959), 24–26.

The Fourth Oasis: The Savior's Victory

30. C.S. Lewis, *The Lion, the Witch, and the Wardrobe* (New York: Harper Trophy, 1978), 168, 170, 178.

31. Walter Wink, as quoted in Philip Yancey, *The Jesus I Never Knew*, 284.

32. Elisabeth Elliot, *A Chance to Die: The Life and Legacy of Amy Carmichael* (Grand Rapids: Revell, 1987), 64.

33. Darrell L. Bock, *Luke*. Vol. 2, 1706.

34. Luci Shaw, *God in the Dark: Through Grief and Beyond* (Grand Rapids: Broadmoor, 1989), 63.

35. H.D.M. Spence, "Luke." *The Pulpit Commentary*, 197–98.

36. C.S. Lewis, *The Screwtape Letters & Screwtape Proposes a Toast* (New York: Macmillan, 1961), 3.

37. Ken Gire, *Intimate Moments with the Savior: Learning to Love*, 98.

38. Max Lucado, *The Applause of Heaven* (Dallas: Word, 1996).

39. Darrell L. Bock, *Luke*. Vol. 2, 1867.

40. C.S. Lewis, *Mere Christianity* (New York: Macmillan, 1964), 40–41.

41. C.S. Lewis, *The Lion, the Witch, and the Wardrobe*, 51–52.

42. Matthew Henry, "Matthew to John." *Matthew Henry's Commentary on the Whole Bible*. Vol. 5. (Peabody, Mass.: Hendrickson, 1991), 963.

43. Darrell L. Bock, *Luke*. Vol. 2, 1845.

44. H.D.M. Spence, *"Luke."* The Pulpit Commentary, 185.

45. Darrell L. Bock, *Luke*. Vol. 2, 1875.

46. Philip Yancey, *The Jesus I Never Knew*, 212–13.

47. Flavius Josephus, "The Antiquities of the Jews." *Josephus: Complete Works*, trans. by William Whiston (Grand Rapids: Kregel, 1981), 97.

48. Philip Yancey, *The Jesus I Never Knew*, 212.

49. A. Plummer, as quoted in Darrell L. Bock, *Luke*. Vol. 2, 1898.

50. Walter Wangerin, Jr., *The Book of God: The Bible as a Novel*, 822–23.

51. Billy Graham, *Just As I Am: The Autobiography of Billy Graham*, 668.

52. Darrell L. Bock, *Luke*. Vol. 2, 1923.